CLASSIC
CHINESE
COOKING

CLASSIC
CHINESE
COOKING

TEMPTING TASTES
FROM THE EAST

Consultant Editor: Linda Doeser

Sebastian Kelly

First published in 1999 by Sebastian Kelly
2 Rectory Road, Oxford 0X4 1BW

© Anness Publishing Limited 1999

Produced by Anness Publishing Limited
Hermes House, 88-89 Blackfriars Road
London SE1 8HA

ISBN 1 84081 154 4

A CIP catalogue record for this book is available from the British Library

Publisher: Joanna Lorenz
Project Editor: Linda Doeser
Copy Editor: Harriet Lanzer
Designers: Ian Sandom, Siân Keogh
Illustrator: Madeleine David

Front cover: Lisa Tai, Designer; Thomas Odulate, Photographer;
Helen Trent, Stylist; Lucy McKelvie, Home Economist

Photography: Karl Adamson, Edward Allwright, David Armstrong, Steve Baxter,
James Duncan, Michelle Garrett, Amanda Heywood, Patrick McLeavey,
William Lingwood, Michael Michaels and Thomas Odulate
Additional recipes: Kathy Man
Styling: Madeleine Brehaut, Michelle Garrett, Claire Lousie Hunt, Maria Kelly,
Blake Minton and Kirsty Rawlings
Food for Photography: Carla Capalbo, Kit Chan, Joanne Craig, Nicola Fowler,
Carole Handslip, Jane Hartshorn, Wendy Lee, Lucy McKelvie, Annie Nichols,
Jane Stevenson, Steven Wheeler and Elizabeth Wolf-Cohen

Previously published as part of a larger compendium, *The Ultimate Chinese & Asian Cookbook*

Printed and bound in Hong Kong/China

1 3 5 7 9 10 8 6 4 2

NOTES
For all recipes, quantities are given in both metric and imperial measures and,
where appropriate, measures are given in standard cups and spoons. Follow one
set, but not a mixture, as they are not interchangeable.
Standard spoon and cup measurements are level.
1 tsp = 5ml; 1 tbsp = 15ml; 1 cup = 250ml/8fl oz
Australian standard tablespoons are 20ml. Australian readers should use 3 tsp in
place of 1 tbsp for measuring small quantities of gelatine, cornflour, salt, etc.
Medium eggs should be used unless otherwise stated.

CONTENTS

INTRODUCTION

China is a vast country with many different regions. For nearly one thousand years, the northern city of Peking (now Beijing) has been the capital. Visiting dignitaries brought their chefs and culinary traditions from other parts of China. Through a mixture of co-operation and rivalry, they developed a light and elegant *haute cuisine*. Peking Duck must be the best-known speciality of the region.

Cantonese cooking in the South is colourful and sophisticated, based on abundant fresh vegetables, fish and seafood. Stir-frying was perfected here, and Canton is the home of Dim Sum, which literally means "to please the heart", and this describes the Cantonese approach to food.

Eastern Chinese cuisine divides into several styles. North of the Yangtze delta is famous for noodles and dumplings and is the home of the renowned Lion's Head Casserole. The southern provinces are known as the "Land of Fish and Rice", although their cuisine also includes many duck and pork dishes. The port of Shanghai has a unique style, influenced by the West as well as many parts of China.

The cuisine of Szechuan in the West of China is well-known for its superb balance of spices and aromatic flavourings. Chillies and Szechuan peppercorns are important and dishes are typically piquant and full of zest.

What all the classic dishes of the regional cuisines have in common is a harmonious balance of flavours, colours and textures and a long tradition of excellence.

THE WOK

There are many different varieties of wok available. All are bowl-shaped with gently sloping sides that allow the heat to spread rapidly and evenly over the surface. One that is about 35cm/14in in diameter is a useful size for most families, allowing adequate room for deep frying, steaming and braising, as well as stir-frying.

Originally always made from cast iron, woks are now manufactured in a number of different metals. Cast iron remains very popular as it is an excellent conductor of heat and develops a patina over a period of time that makes it virtually non-stick. Carbon steel is also a good choice, but stainless steel tends to scorch. Non-stick woks are available but are not really very efficient because they cannot withstand the high heat required for wok cooking. They are also expensive.

Woks may have an ear-shaped handle made from metal or wood, a single long handle or both. Wooden handles are safer.

SEASONING THE WOK

New woks, apart from those with a non-stick lining, must be seasoned. Many need to be scrubbed first with a cream cleanser to remove the manufacturer's protective coating of oil. Once the oil has been removed, place the wok over a low heat and add about 30ml/2 tbsp vegetable oil. Rub the oil over the entire inside surface of the wok with a pad of kitchen paper. Heat the wok slowly for 10–15 minutes, then wipe off the oil with more kitchen paper. The paper will become black. Repeat this process of coating, heating and wiping several times until the paper is clean.

Once the wok has been seasoned, it should not be scrubbed again. After use, just wash it in hot water without using any detergent, then wipe it completely dry before storage. A wok in frequent use will not rust. However, if it does, scour off the rust and repeat the seasoning process.

WOK ACCESSORIES

There is a range of accessories available to go with woks, but they are by no means essential.

LID

This is a useful addition, particularly if you want to use the wok for steaming and braising, as well as frying. Usually made of aluminium, it is a close-fitting, dome-shaped cover. Some woks are sold already supplied with matching lids. However, any snug-fitting, dome-shaped saucepan lid is an adequate substitute.

STAND

This is used to provide a secure base for the wok when it is used for steaming, braising or deep frying and is a particularly useful accessory. Stands are always made of metal but vary in form, usually either a simple open-sided frame or a solid metal ring with holes punched around the sides.

TRIVET

This is essential for steaming to support the plate above the water level. Trivets are made of wood or metal.

SCOOP

This is a long, often wooden-handled metal spatula with a wooden end used to toss ingredients during stir-frying. Any good, long-handled spoon can be used instead, although it does not have quite the same action.

Additional equipment is not essential for cooking with a wok, but utensils designed with this in mind – and tried and tested through time – can sometimes make the process easier. Wire and stainless steel skimmers, a wok scoop, a trivet and a selection of bamboo steamers in various sizes are among the most useful. Chinese cleavers are beautifully balanced cutting tools that can be used for both coarse and fine chopping. However, the range of cooking equipment found in most western kitchens can usually provide adequate substitutes for traditional Chinese tools and utensils.

WOK BRUSH

This bundle of stiff split bamboo is used for cleaning the wok. An ordinary kitchen brush is quite adequate.

OTHER EQUIPMENT

Most equipment required for cooking the recipes in this book will be found in any kitchen. Any specialist tools are generally simple and inexpensive, especially if you seek out authentic implements from oriental stores.

BAMBOO STEAMER

This fits inside the wok where it should rest safely perched on the

sloping sides. Bamboo steamers range in size from small for dumplings and dim sum to those large enough to hold a whole fish.

BAMBOO STRAINER
This wide, flat metal strainer with a long bamboo handle makes lifting foods from steam or hot oil easier. A slotted metal spoon can also be used.

CHOPSTICKS
Extra long wooden chopsticks are useful for stirring, fluffing up rice, separating noodles during cooking and turning and transferring items.

CLEAVER
No Chinese cook would be without one. This is an all-purpose cutting tool, available in various weights and sizes. It is easy to use and serves many purposes from chopping up bones to precision cutting, such as deveining prawns. It is a superb instrument for thinly slicing vegetables. It must be kept very sharp.

CHINESE GRATER
These are typically made of wood.

BALTI PAN
Also called a karahi, this is the Balti equivalent of a wok and is used in much the same way. A new Balti pan should be seasoned in the same way as a new wok.

PESTLE AND MORTAR
Usually made of earthenware, this is extremely useful for grinding small amounts of spices and for pounding ingredients together to make pastes.

FOOD PROCESSOR
This is a quick and easy alternative to the pestle and mortar for grinding spices. It can also be used for chopping and slicing vegetables.

COOKING TECHNIQUES

STIR-FRYING

This quick technique retains the fresh flavour, colour and texture of ingredients and its success depends upon having all that you require ready prepared before starting to cook.

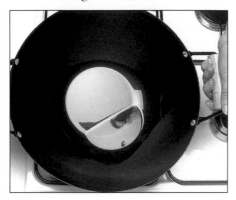

1 Heat an empty wok over a high heat. This prevents food sticking and will ensure an even heat. Add the oil and swirl it around so that it coats the base and halfway up the sides of the wok. It is important that the oil is hot when the food is added, so that it will start to cook immediately.

2 Add the ingredients in the order specified in the recipe: usually aromatics first (garlic, ginger, spring onions). If this is the case, do not wait for the oil to get so hot that it is almost smoking or they will burn and become bitter. Toss them in the oil for a few seconds. Next add the main ingredients that require longer cooking, such as dense vegetables or meat. Follow with the faster-cooking items. Toss the ingredients from the centre of the wok to the sides using a wok scoop, long-handled spoon or wooden spatula.

DEEP FRYING

A wok is ideal for deep frying as it uses far less oil than a deep fat fryer. Make sure that it is fully secure on its stand before adding the oil and never leave the wok unattended.

1 Put the wok on a stand and half fill with oil. Heat until the required temperature registers on a thermometer. Alternatively, test it by dropping in a small piece of food; if bubbles form all over the surface of the food, the oil is ready.

2 Carefully add the food to the oil, using long wooden chopsticks or tongs, and move it around to prevent it sticking together. Use a bamboo strainer or slotted spoon to remove the food. Drain on kitchen paper before serving.

STEAMING

Steamed foods are cooked by a gentle, moist heat which must circulate freely in order for the food to cook. Steaming is increasingly popular with health-conscious cooks as it preserves flavour and nutrients. It is perfect for vegetables, meat, poultry and especially fish. The easiest way to steam food in a wok is using a bamboo steamer.

USING A BAMBOO STEAMER

1 Put the wok on a stand. Pour in sufficient boiling water to come about 5cm/2in up the sides and bring back to simmering point. Carefully put the bamboo steamer into the wok so that it rests securely against the sloping sides without touching the surface of the water.

2 Cover the steamer with its matching lid and cook for the time recommended in the recipe. Check the water level from time to time and top up with boiling water if necessary.

USING A WOK AS A STEAMER

1 Put a trivet in the wok, then place the wok securely on its stand. Pour in sufficient boiling water to come just below the trivet. Carefully place a plate containing the food to be steamed on the trivet.

2 Cover the wok with its lid, bring the water back to the boil, then lower the heat so that it is simmering gently. Steam for the time recommended in the recipe. Check the water level from time to time and top up with boiling water if necessary.

INGREDIENTS

BAMBOO SHOOTS
These mild-flavoured tender shoots of the young bamboo are widely available fresh or sliced or halved in cans.

BEANSPROUTS
These shoots of the mung bean are usually available from supermarkets. They add a crisp texture to stir-fries.

1 Pick over the beansprouts and discard any that are discoloured, broken or wilted.

2 Rinse the beansprouts under cold running water and drain well.

CHINESE FIVE-SPICE POWDER
This flavouring contains star anise, pepper, fennel, cloves and cinnamon.

CHINESE PANCAKES
These unseasoned, flour-and-water pancakes are available fresh or frozen.

CHINESE RICE WINE
It has a rich, sherry-like flavour and can be found in most large super-markets and oriental food stores. Sherry may be used as a substitute.

CREAMED COCONUT
This is available in a solid block from oriental food stores and large super-markets. It gives an intense coconut flavour; simply add water to make a thick coconut paste. It can be thinned with more water if required.

GINGER
Ginger has a sharp distinctive flavour. Choose firm, plump pieces of fresh root with unwrinkled, shiny skins.

1 Using a small sharp knife, peel the skin from the root.

2 Place the ginger on a board. Set the flat side of a cleaver or chef's knife on top and strike it firmly with your fist to soften its fibrous texture.

3 Chop the ginger as coarsely or finely as you wish, moving the blade backwards and forwards.

GRAM FLOUR
Made from ground chick-peas, this flour has a unique flavour and is worth seeking out in Indian food stores.

KAFFIR LIME LEAVES
These are used rather like bay leaves, but to give an aromatic lime flavour to dishes. The fresh leaves are available from oriental food stores and can be frozen for future use.

1 Using a small sharp knife, remove the centre vein.

2 Cut the leaves crossways into very fine strips.

LEMON GRASS
This herb imparts a mild, sour-sweet, citrus flavour. Split and use whole, finely chopped or ground to a paste.

MOOLI
Mooli is a member of the radish family with a fresh, slightly peppery taste. Unlike other radishes, it is good when cooked, but should be salted and allowed to drain first, as it has a high water content. It is widely used in Chinese cooking and may be carved into an elaborate garnish.

OKRA
This edible seed pod is a member of the hibiscus family and is also known as bhindi, gumbo and ladies' fingers. It is widely used in Indian cuisine.

OYSTER SAUCE
Made from oyster extract, it is used in many fish dishes, soups and sauces.

PLUM SAUCE
This is a sweet and sour sauce with a unique fruity flavour.

RED BEAN PASTE
This reddish-brown paste is made from puréed red beans and crystallized sugar. It is usually sold in cans.

RICE
Long grain rice is generally used for savoury dishes. There are many high-quality varieties, coming from a range of countries. Basmati, which means fragrant in Hindi, is generally acknowl-edged as the prince or king of rices and is probably the ideal choice for Balti recipes that suggest serving the dish with it. Thai jasmine rice is also fragrant and slightly sticky.

RICE WINE
Made from glutinous rice, Chinese rice wine is also known as yellow wine – *Huang Jiu* or *Chiew* – because of its colour. The best variety is called *Shao Hsing* or *Shaoxing* and comes from the south-east of China. Dry or medium sherry may be used as substitute.

SALTED BLACK BEANS
Sold in plastic bags and jars, these very

salty and pungent beans should be crushed with water or wine before use. They will keep almost indefinitely in a screw-top jar.

SESAME OIL

This is used more for flavouring than for cooking. It is very intensely flavoured so only a little is required.

SHALLOTS

Mild-flavoured members of the onion family, shallots are used in many flavourings and sauces. Fried in crisp flakes, they can be used as a garnish.

SPRING ONIONS

These are widely used in stir-fried dishes. The thinner the onion, the milder it will be. Chop off any roots and the top part of the green section, then chop finely or cut into matchstick strips. In some recipes, the green and white parts are kept separate for an extra decorative effect.

Cockwise from top left yellow bean sauce, black bean sauce, oyster sauce, dark soy sauce, light soy sauce and hoisin sauce.

Remove and discard the woody stalks from soaked, dried Chinese mushrooms, then use the caps whole, sliced or chopped.

SHIITAKE MUSHROOMS

Dried shiitake mushrooms, widely known as Chinese dried mushrooms, are frequently used in classic Chinese cuisine. They have a more concentrated flavour than fresh mushrooms. They should be soaked in hot water before use for about 30 minutes, until softened. Remove and discard the stalks and use the caps whole, sliced or chopped, according to the recipe.

SOY SAUCE

Made from the naturally fermented soya bean, this is an important ingredient in Chinese cooking. There are two types: dark and light. Dark soy sauce is rich and used to add both colour and flavour to many sauces and marinades. It is quite salty and is often used instead of salt to season a dish. Light soy sauce is thinner, lighter and has a fresher taste than dark. It is also saltier. It is used in cooking, as a table condiment and as a dipping sauce.

SPRING ROLL SKINS OR WRAPPERS

Paper-thin wrappers made from wheat or rice flour and water, they are available from Chinese supermarkets. Wheat wrappers are usually sold frozen and should be thawed and separated before use. Rice flour wrappers are dry and must be soaked before use.

STRAW MUSHROOMS

These are grown on rice straw and have a slippery texture, for which they are prized, but little flavour. They are available canned from supermarkets and Chinese food stores. They are not widely available fresh in the West.

Often used to add texture and colour contrast in stir-fried meat and fish dishes, wood ears must be soaked before use. Then discard the woody stems and slice thinly.

WATER CHESTNUTS
This walnut-size bulb comes from an Asian water plant and looks like a sweet chestnut, although the two plants are not related. They are sold fresh by some Chinese supermarkets, but are usually more readily available canned.

WONTON WRAPPERS
These paper-thin squares of yellow-coloured dough are available from most Chinese supermarkets.

WOOD EARS
Dried edible fungi that have a crunchy texture, wood ears are widely available from Chinese supermarkets. Cloud ears, which are similar but with a more delicate flavour, are sometimes a little more difficult to obtain. Once reconstituted in water, they expand to many times their original size. They should be soaked in hot water before use for 30 minutes, or until softened. Drain, rinse and cut them into small pieces, discarding the tough base.

YELLOW BEAN SAUCE
This thick paste is made from salted, fermented, yellow soya beans, crushed with flour and sugar.

SZECHUAN PEPPERCORNS
Also known as farchiew, these aromatic red peppercorns are best used roasted and ground. They are not so hot as either white or black peppercorns, but do add a unique taste to food.

TOFU
Also known as bean curd, tofu is used extensively in Chinese cooking and is a good source of protein, especially for vegetarians. Although it is very bland, indeed almost flavourless, tofu readily absorbs the flavours of the food with which it is cooked. Firm blocks of tofu are best suited to stir-frying. Store, covered with water, in the refrigerator.

Clockwise from top: fresh bean curd or tofu, dried bean curd sticks and aduki beans – just some of the protein-rich components of many Chinese recipes.

Tofu is readily available from supermarkets and health food stores. There are several other different types of tofu, including "silken" and smoked. Dried bean curd sticks are sheets of tofu that have been formed into sticks and dried. They are an important ingredient in Chinese vegetarian dishes. They must be soaked in hot water before being used. Bean curd sticks are usually available from Chinese food stores.

SOUPS &
STARTERS

Chicken Wonton Soup with Prawns

This soup is a more luxurious version of the familiar, basic Wonton Soup and is almost a meal in itself.

INGREDIENTS

Serves 4

275g/10oz boneless chicken
  breast, skinned
200g/7oz prawn tails, raw or cooked
5ml/1 tsp finely chopped fresh root
  ginger
2 spring onions, finely chopped
1 egg
10ml/2 tsp oyster sauce (optional)
1 packet wonton wrappers
15ml/1 tbsp cornflour paste
900ml/1½ pints/3¾ cups chicken stock
¼ cucumber, peeled and diced
salt and ground black pepper
1 spring onion, roughly shredded,
  4 sprigs fresh coriander and 1 tomato,
  skinned, seeded and diced, to garnish

1 Place the chicken breast, 150g/5oz of the prawn tails, the ginger and spring onions in a food processor and process for 2–3 minutes. Add the egg, oyster sauce and seasoning and process briefly. Set aside.

2 Place 8 wonton wrappers at a time on a surface, moisten the edges with cornflour paste and place 2.5ml/ ½ tsp of the chicken and prawn mixture in the centre of each. Fold them in half and pinch to seal. Simmer in salted water for 4 minutes.

3 Bring the chicken stock to the boil, add the remaining prawn tails and the cucumber and simmer for 3–4 minutes. Add the filled wontons and simmer for 3–4 minutes to warm through. Garnish with the spring onion, coriander and diced tomato and serve hot.

Sweetcorn and Chicken Soup

This popular classic Chinese soup is delicious and extremely easy to make in a wok.

INGREDIENTS

Serves 4–6

1 chicken breast fillet, about 115g/
    4oz, skinned and cubed
10ml/2 tsp light soy sauce
15ml/1 tbsp Chinese rice wine or
    dry sherry
5ml/1 tsp cornflour
60ml/4 tbsp cold water
5ml/ 1 tsp sesame oil
30ml/2 tbsp groundnut oil
5ml/1 tsp grated fresh root ginger
1 litre/1³/₄ pints/4 cups chicken stock
425g/15oz can creamed sweetcorn
225g/8oz can sweetcorn kernels
2 eggs, beaten
salt and ground black pepper
2–3 spring onions, green parts only, cut
    into tiny rounds, to garnish

1 Mince the chicken in a food processor or blender, taking care not to over-process. Transfer the chicken to a bowl and stir in the soy sauce, rice wine or sherry, cornflour, water, sesame oil and seasoning. Cover and leave for about 15 minutes to absorb the flavours.

2 Heat a wok over a medium heat. Add the groundnut oil and swirl it around. Add the ginger and stir-fry for a few seconds. Add the stock, creamed sweetcorn and sweetcorn kernels. Bring to just below boiling point.

3 Spoon about 90ml/6 tbsp of the hot liquid into the chicken mixture and stir until it forms a smooth paste. Add to the wok. Slowly bring to the boil, stirring constantly, then simmer for 2–3 minutes until cooked.

4 Pour the beaten eggs into the soup in a slow, steady stream, using a fork or chopsticks to stir the top of the soup in a figure-of-eight pattern. The egg should set in lacy threads. Serve immediately with the spring onions sprinkled over.

Beef Noodle Soup

A steaming bowl, packed with delicious flavours and a taste of the Orient, will be welcome on cold winter days.

INGREDIENTS

Serves 4

10g/¼oz dried porcini mushrooms
150 ml/¼ pint/⅔ cup boiling water
6 spring onions
115g/4oz carrots
350g/12oz rump steak
about 30 ml/2 tbsp sunflower oil
1 garlic clove, crushed
2.5 cm/1in piece fresh root ginger,
   peeled and finely chopped
1.2 litres/2 pints /5 cups beef stock
45 ml/3 tbsp light soy sauce
60 ml/4 tbsp Chinese rice wine or
   dry sherry
75g/3oz thin egg noodles
75g/3oz spinach, shredded
salt and ground black pepper

3 Heat the oil in a large saucepan and cook the beef in batches until browned, adding a little more oil if necessary. Remove the beef with a slotted spoon and set aside to drain on kitchen paper.

4 Add the garlic, ginger, spring onions and carrots to the pan and stir-fry for 3 minutes.

5 Add the beef stock, the mushrooms and their soaking liquid, the soy sauce, rice wine or dry sherry and plenty of seasoning. Bring to the boil and simmer, covered, for 10 minutes.

6 Break up the noodles slightly and add to the pan, with the spinach. Simmer gently for 5 minutes, or until the beef is tender. Adjust the seasoning before serving.

1 Break the mushrooms into small pieces, place in a bowl and pour over the boiling water. Set aside to soak for 15 minutes.

2 Shred the spring onions and carrots into 5cm/2in-long fine strips. Trim any fat off the rump steak and slice into thin strips.

Clear Soup with Meatballs

INGREDIENTS

Serves 8

For the meatballs
175g/6oz very finely minced beef
1 small onion, very finely chopped
1–2 garlic cloves, crushed
15ml/1 tbsp cornflour
a little egg white, lightly beaten
salt and freshly ground black pepper

For the soup
4–6 Chinese mushrooms, soaked in
   warm water for 30 minutes
30ml/2 tbsp groundnut oil
1 large onion, finely chopped
2 garlic cloves, finely crushed
1cm/½ in fresh root ginger, bruised
2 litres/3½ pints/8 cups beef or
   chicken stock, including soaking
   liquid from the mushrooms
30ml/2 tbsp soy sauce
115g/4oz curly kale, spinach or
   Chinese leaves, shredded

1 First prepare the meatballs. Mix the beef with the onion, garlic, cornflour and seasoning in a food processor and then bind with sufficient egg white to make a firm mixture. With wetted hands, roll into tiny, bite-size balls and set aside.

2 Drain the mushrooms and reserve the soaking liquid to add to the stock. Trim off and discard the stalks. Slice the caps finely and set aside.

3 Heat a wok or large saucepan and add the oil. Fry the onion, garlic and ginger to bring out the flavour, but do not allow to brown.

4 When the onion is soft, pour in the stock. Bring to the boil, then stir in the soy sauce and mushroom slices and simmer for 10 minutes. Add the meatballs and cook for 10 minutes.

5 Just before serving, remove the ginger. Stir in the shredded curly kale, spinach or Chinese leaves. Heat through for 1 minute only: no longer or the leaves will be overcooked. Serve the soup immediately.

Chicken and Asparagus Soup

This is a very delicate and delicious soup, with chicken and asparagus simply and quickly prepared in a wok.

INGREDIENTS

Serves 4

150g/5oz chicken breast fillet
5ml/1 tsp egg white
5ml/1 tsp cornflour paste
115g/4oz fresh or canned asparagus
750ml/1¼ pints/3 cups stock
salt and ground black pepper
fresh coriander leaves, to garnish

1 Cut the chicken meat into thin slices, each about the size of a postage stamp. Mix with a pinch of salt, then add the egg white and finally the cornflour paste.

2 Discard the tough stems of the asparagus, and cut the tender spears diagonally into short lengths.

3 Bring the stock to a rolling boil in a wok. Add the asparagus, bring back to the boil and cook for 2 minutes. (This is not necessary if you are using canned asparagus.)

4 Add the chicken, stir to separate and bring back to the boil once more. Adjust the seasoning to taste. Serve hot, garnished with fresh coriander leaves.

Crab Spring Rolls and Dipping Sauce

Chilli and grated ginger add a hint of heat to these sensational treats. Serve them as a starter or with other Chinese dishes as part of a main course.

INGREDIENTS

Serves 4–6
15ml/1 tbsp groundnut oil
5ml/1 tsp sesame oil
1 garlic clove, crushed
1 fresh red chilli, seeded and finely sliced
450g/1lb fresh stir-fry vegetables, such as beansprouts and shredded carrots, peppers and mangetouts
30ml/2 tbsp chopped coriander
2.5cm/1in piece of fresh root ginger, grated
15ml/1 tbsp Chinese rice wine or dry sherry
15ml/1 tbsp soy sauce
350g/12oz fresh dressed crab meat (brown and white meat)
12 spring roll wrappers
1 small egg, beaten
oil, for deep-frying
salt and ground black pepper
lime wedges and fresh coriander, to garnish

For the dipping sauce
1 onion, thinly sliced
oil, for deep-frying
1 fresh red chilli, seeded and finely chopped
2 garlic cloves, crushed
60ml/4 tbsp dark soy sauce
20ml/4 tsp lemon juice or 15–25ml/1–1½ tbsp prepared tamarind juice
30ml/2 tbsp hot water

1 First make the sauce. Spread the onion out on kitchen paper and leave to dry for 30 minutes. Then half-fill a wok with oil and heat to 190°C/375°F. Fry the onion in batches until crisp and golden, turning all the time. Drain on kitchen paper.

2 Mix together the chilli, garlic, soy sauce, lemon or tamarind juice and hot water in a bowl.

3 Stir in the onion and leave to stand for 30 minutes.

4 Heat the groundnut and sesame oils in a clean, preheated wok. When hot, stir-fry the crushed garlic and chilli for 1 minute. Add the vegetables, coriander and ginger and stir-fry for 1 minute more. Drizzle over the rice wine or dry sherry and soy sauce. Allow the mixture to bubble up for 1 minute.

5 Using a slotted spoon, transfer the vegetables to a bowl. Set aside until cool, then stir in the crab meat and season with salt and pepper.

6 Soften the spring roll wrappers, following the directions on the packet. Place some of the filling on a wrapper, fold over the front edge and the sides and roll up neatly, sealing the edges with a little beaten egg. Repeat with the remaining wrappers and filling.

7 Heat the oil for deep-frying in the wok and fry the spring rolls in batches, turning several times, until brown and crisp. Remove with a slotted spoon, drain on kitchen paper and keep hot while frying the remainder. Serve at once, garnished with lime wedges and coriander, with the dipping sauce.

Butterfly Prawns

For best results, use uncooked giant or king prawns in their shells for this deep fried dish. Sold headless, they are about 8–10cm/3–4in long, and you should get 18–20 prawns per 450g/1lb.

Ingredients

Serves 6–8

450g/1lb uncooked prawns in their
   shells, headless
5ml/1 tsp ground Szechuan
   peppercorns
15ml/1 tbsp light soy sauce
15ml/1 tbsp Chinese rice wine or
   dry sherry
10ml/2 tsp cornflour
2 eggs, lightly beaten
60–75ml/4–5 tbsp breadcrumbs
vegetable oil, for deep frying
2–3 spring onions, to garnish
lettuce leaves or crispy "seaweed",
   to serve

1 Peel the prawns but leave the tails on. Split the prawns in half from the underbelly, about three-quarters of the way through, leaving the tails still firmly attached.

2 Put the prawns in a bowl with the pepper, soy sauce, rice wine or sherry and cornflour and set aside to marinate for 10–15 minutes.

3 Pick up one prawn at a time by the tail, and dip it in the beaten egg.

4 Roll the egg-covered prawns in breadcrumbs.

5 Heat the oil in a wok until medium-hot. Gently lower the prawns into the oil.

6 Deep fry the prawns in batches until golden brown. Remove and drain. Garnish with spring onions, which are either raw or have been soaked for about 30 seconds in hot oil. To serve, arrange the prawns neatly on a bed of lettuce leaves or crispy "seaweed".

Steamed Pork and Water Chestnut Wontons

Ginger and Chinese five-spice powder flavour this version of steamed dumplings – a favourite snack in many teahouses.

INGREDIENTS

Makes about 36
2 large Chinese cabbage leaves, plus
    extra for lining the steamer
2 spring onions, finely chopped
1cm/½in fresh root ginger, chopped
50g/2oz canned water chestnuts, rinsed
    and finely chopped
225g/8oz minced pork
2.5ml/½ tsp Chinese five-spice powder
15ml/1 tbsp cornflour
15ml/1 tbsp light soy sauce
15ml/1 tbsp Chinese rice wine or
    dry sherry
10ml/2 tsp sesame oil
generous pinch of caster sugar
about 36 wonton wrappers, each
    7.5cm/3in square
light soy sauce and hot chilli oil,
    for dipping

1 Place the Chinese cabbage leaves on top of one another. Cut them lengthways into quarters and then across into thin shreds.

2 Place the shredded Chinese cabbage leaves in a bowl. Add the spring onions, ginger, water chestnuts, pork, five-spice powder, cornflour, soy sauce, rice wine or dry sherry, sesame oil and sugar and mix well.

3 Place a heaped teaspoon of the filling in the centre of the wrapper. Lightly dampen the edges with water.

4 Lift the wrapper up around the filling, gathering it to form a "purse". Squeeze the wrapper firmly around the middle, then tap the bottom to make a flat base. The top should be open. Place the wonton on a tray and cover with a damp tea towel. Repeat.

5 Line a steamer with cabbage leaves and steam the dumplings for 12–15 minutes, until tender. Remove each batch from the steamer as soon they are cooked, cover with foil and keep warm. Serve hot with soy sauce and chilli oil for dipping.

Dim Sum

Popular as a snack in China, these tiny dumplings are fast becoming fashionable in many fast-food, as well as specialist, restaurants in the West.

INGREDIENTS

Serves 4
For the dough
150g/5oz/1¼ cups plain flour
50ml/2fl oz/¼ cup boiling water
25ml/1½ tbsp cold water
7.5ml/½ tbsp vegetable oil

For the filling
75g/3oz minced pork
45ml/3 tbsp canned chopped
  bamboo shoots
7.5ml/½ tbsp light soy sauce
5ml/1 tsp dry sherry
5ml/1 tsp demerara sugar
2.5ml/½ tsp sesame oil
5ml/1 tsp cornflour
lettuce leaves such as iceberg, frisée or
  Webbs, soy sauce, spring onion curls,
  sliced fresh red chilli and prawn
  crackers, to serve

1 To make the dough, sift the flour into a bowl. Stir in the boiling water, then the cold water together with the oil. Mix to form a dough and knead until smooth.

2 Divide the mixture into 16 equal pieces and shape into circles.

3 For the filling, mix together the pork, bamboo shoots, soy sauce, dry sherry, sugar and oil.

4 Add the cornflour and stir well until thoroughly combined.

5 Place a little of the filling in the centre of each dim sum circle. Pinch the edges of the dough together to form little "purses".

6 Line a steamer with a damp tea towel. Place the dim sum in the steamer and steam for 5–10 minutes. Arrange the lettuce leaves on four individual serving plates, top with the dim sum and serve with soy sauce, spring onion curls, sliced red chilli and prawn crackers.

VARIATION

You can replace the pork with cooked, peeled prawns. Sprinkle 15ml/1 tbsp sesame seeds on to the dim sum before cooking, if wished.

Deep-fried Ribs with Spicy Salt and Pepper

INGREDIENTS

Serves 4–6
10–12 finger ribs, about 675g/1½lb, with excess fat and gristle trimmed
about 30–45ml/2–3 tbsp flour
vegetable oil, for deep frying

For the marinade
1 clove garlic, crushed and finely chopped
15ml/1 tbsp light brown sugar
15ml/1 tbsp light soy sauce
15ml/1 tbsp dark soy sauce
30ml/2 tbsp Chinese rice wine or dry sherry
2.5ml/½ tsp chilli sauce
few drops sesame oil

For the spicy salt and pepper
15ml/1 tbsp salt
10ml/2 tsp ground Szechuan peppercorns
5ml/1 tsp five-spice powder

1 Chop each rib into three or four pieces, then mix with all the marinade ingredients and marinate for at least 2–3 hours.

2 Coat the ribs with flour and deep fry in medium-hot oil for 4–5 minutes, stirring to separate. Remove from the oil and drain.

COOK'S TIP

Ideally, each sparerib should be chopped into three or four bite-sized pieces before or after deep frying in a wok. If this is not possible, then serve the ribs whole.

3 Heat the oil to high and deep fry the ribs once more for about 1 minute, or until the colour is an even dark brown. Remove and drain.

4 To make the spicy salt and pepper, heat all the ingredients in a preheated dry wok for about 2 minutes over a low heat, stirring constantly. Serve with the ribs.

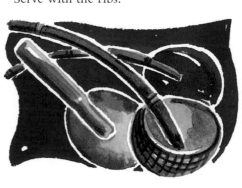

Bon-bon Chicken with Sesame Sauce

The chicken meat is tenderized by being beaten with a stick (called a *bon* in Chinese), hence the name for this very popular Szechuan dish.

INGREDIENTS

Serves 6–8
1 chicken, about 1kg/2¼lb
1.2 litre/2 pints/5 cups water
15ml/1 tbsp sesame oil
shredded cucumber, to garnish

For the sauce
30ml/2 tbsp light soy sauce
5ml/1 tsp sugar
15ml/1 tbsp finely chopped
    spring onions
5ml/1 tsp red chilli oil
2.5ml/½ tsp ground Szechuan
    peppercorns
5ml/1 tsp white sesame seeds
30ml/2 tbsp sesame paste or 30ml/
    2 tbsp peanut butter creamed with a
    little sesame oil

1 Clean the chicken well. Bring the water to a rolling boil in a wok, add the chicken. Reduce the heat, cover and cook for 40–45 minutes. Remove the chicken and immerse in cold water to cool.

2 After at least 1 hour, remove the chicken and drain; dry well with kitchen paper and brush on a coating of sesame oil. Carve the meat off the legs, wings and breast and pull the meat off the rest of the bones.

3 On a flat surface, pound the meat with a rolling pin, then tear the meat into shreds with your fingers.

4 Place the meat in a dish with the shredded cucumber around the edge. In a bowl, mix together all the sauce ingredients, keeping a few spring onions to garnish. Pour the sauce over the chicken and serve.

FISH &
SEAFOOD

Gong Boa Prawns

This pleasantly spicy sweet-and-sour prawn dish takes only minutes to make.

INGREDIENTS

Serves 4

350g/12oz raw tiger prawns
½ cucumber, about 75g/3oz
300ml/½ pint/1¼ cups fish stock
15ml/1 tbsp vegetable oil
2.5ml/½ tsp crushed dried chillies
½ green pepper, seeded and cut into
   2.5cm/1in strips
1 small carrot, thinly sliced
30ml/2 tbsp tomato ketchup
45ml/3 tbsp rice vinegar
15ml/1 tbsp caster sugar
150ml/¼ pint/⅔ cup vegetable stock
50g/2oz/½ cup drained canned
   pineapple chunks
10ml/2 tsp cornflour
15ml/1 tbsp cold water
salt

1 Peel and devein the prawns. Rub them gently with 2.5ml/½ tsp salt. Leave them for a few minutes, then wash and dry thoroughly.

2 Pare strips of skin off the cucumber to give a stripy effect. Cut the cucumber in half lengthways and scoop out the seeds with a teaspoon. Cut the flesh into 5mm/¼in crescents.

3 Bring the fish stock to the boil in a saucepan. Add the prawns, lower the heat and poach them for about 2 minutes, until they turn pink. Drain the prawns and set aside.

4 Heat the oil in a preheated wok or frying pan. Add the chillies and stir-fry for a few seconds, then add the pepper strips and carrot slices and stir-fry for 1 minute.

5 Mix together the tomato ketchup, vinegar, sugar and vegetable stock, and season with salt. Pour the mixture into the wok or frying pan and cook for 3 minutes.

6 Add the prawns, cucumber and pineapple and cook for 2 minutes. Mix together the cornflour and water to a smooth paste. Add the mixture to the wok or pan and cook, stirring constantly, until the sauce has thickened. Serve immediately.

Baked Crab with Spring Onions and Ginger

This recipe is far less complicated than it looks and will delight the eyes as much as the taste buds.

INGREDIENTS

Serves 4

1 large or 2 medium crabs, about
  675g/1½lb in total
30ml/2 tbsp Chinese rice wine or
  dry sherry
1 egg, lightly beaten
15ml/1 tbsp cornflour
45–60/3–4 tbsp vegetable oil
15ml/1 tbsp finely chopped fresh root
  ginger
3–4 spring onions, cut into short
  lengths
30ml/2 tbsp soy sauce
5ml/1 tsp light brown sugar
about 75ml/5 tbsp Basic Stock
few drops of sesame oil

1 Cut the crab in half from the underbelly. Break off the claws and crack them with the back of a cleaver. Discard the legs and crack the shell, breaking it into several pieces. Discard the feathery gills and the sac. Put the pieces of crab in a bowl.

2 Mix together the rice wine or dry sherry, egg and cornflour and pour over the crab. Leave to marinate for 10–15 minutes.

3 Heat the oil in a preheated wok. Add the crab pieces, ginger and spring onions and stir-fry for about 2–3 minutes.

4 Add the soy sauce, sugar and stock and blend well. Bring to the boil, reduce the heat, cover and braise for 3–4 minutes. Transfer the crab to a serving dish, sprinkle with the sesame oil and serve.

--- COOK'S TIP ---

For the very best flavour, buy a live crab and cook it yourself. However, if you prefer to buy a cooked crab, look for one that feels heavy for its size. This is an indication that it has fully grown into its shell and that there will be plenty of meat. Male crabs have larger claws, so will yield a greater proportion of white meat. However, females – identifiable by a broader, less-pointed tail flap – may contain coral, which many people regard as a delicacy.

Spiced Scallops in their Shells

Scallops are excellent steamed. When served with this spicy sauce, they make a delicious, yet simple, starter for four people or a light lunch for two. Each person spoons sauce on to the scallops before eating them.

INGREDIENTS

Serves 2

8 scallops, shelled (ask the fishmonger to reserve the cupped side of 4 shells)
2 slices fresh root ginger, shredded
½ garlic clove, shredded
2 spring onions, green parts only, shredded
salt and ground black pepper

For the sauce

1 garlic clove, crushed
15ml/1 tbsp grated fresh root ginger
2 spring onions, white parts only, chopped
1–2 fresh green chillies, seeded and finely chopped
15ml/1 tbsp light soy sauce
15ml/1 tbsp dark soy sauce
10ml/2 tsp sesame oil

1 Remove the dark beard-like fringe and tough muscle from the scallops.

2 Place 2 scallops in each shell. Season lightly with salt and pepper, then scatter the ginger, garlic and spring onions on top. Place the shells in a bamboo steamer in a wok and steam for about 6 minutes, until the scallops look opaque (you may have to do this in batches).

3 Meanwhile, make the sauce. Mix together the garlic, ginger, spring onions, chillies, soy sauces and sesame oil and pour into a small serving bowl.

4 Carefully remove each shell from the steamer, taking care not to spill the juices, and arrange them on a serving plate with the sauce bowl in the centre. Serve at once.

Seafood Chow Mein

This basic recipe can be adapted using different items for the "dressing".

INGREDIENTS

Serves 4

75g/3oz squid, cleaned
75g/3oz raw prawns
3–4 fresh scallops
½ egg white
15ml/1 tbsp cornflour paste
250g/9oz egg noodles
75–90ml/5–6 tbsp vegetable oil
50g/2oz mangetouts
2.5ml/½ tsp salt
2.5ml/½ tsp light brown sugar
15ml/1 tbsp Chinese rice wine or
  dry sherry
30ml/2 tbsp light soy sauce
2 spring onions, finely shredded
Basic Stock, if necessary
few drops of sesame oil

1 Open up the squid and score the inside in a criss-cross pattern with a sharp knife. Cut the squid into pieces, each about the size of a postage stamp. Soak the squid in a bowl of boiling water until all the pieces curl up. Rinse in cold water and drain.

2 Peel and devein the prawns, then cut each in half lengthways.

3 Cut each scallop into 3–4 slices. Mix together the scallops, prawns, egg white and cornflour paste.

4 Cook the noodles in boiling water according to the packet instructions. Drain and refresh under cold water. Mix with about 15ml/ 1 tbsp of the oil.

5 Heat 30–45ml/2–3 tbsp of the remaining oil in a preheated wok. Stir-fry the mangetouts, squid and prawn mixture for about 2 minutes, then add the salt, sugar, rice wine or dry sherry, half the soy sauce and the spring onions. Blend well and add a little stock, if necessary. Remove from the wok and keep warm.

6 Heat the remaining oil in the wok and stir-fry the noodles for 2–3 minutes with the remaining soy sauce. Place in a large serving dish, pour the "dressing" on top and sprinkle with a little sesame oil. Serve hot or cold.

Three Sea Flavours Stir-fry

This delectable seafood combination is enhanced by the use of fresh root ginger and spring onions.

INGREDIENTS

Serves 4
4 large scallops with corals
225g/8oz firm white fish fillet, such as monkfish or cod
115g/4oz raw tiger prawns
300ml/½ pint/1¼ cups fish stock
15ml/1 tbsp vegetable oil
2 garlic cloves, coarsely chopped
5cm/2in piece of fresh root ginger, thinly sliced
8 spring onions, cut into 4cm/ 1½in pieces
30ml/2 tbsp Chinese rice wine
5ml/1 tsp cornflour
15ml/1 tbsp water
salt and freshly ground white pepper
noodles, to serve

1 Separate the corals from the scallops and slice each scallop in half horizontally. Cut the fish fillet into bite-size chunks. Peel and devein the tiger prawns.

2 Bring the fish stock to the boil in a saucepan. Add the seafood, lower the heat and poach gently for 1–2 minutes, until the fish, scallops and corals are just firm and the prawns have turned pink. Drain the fish and seafood, reserving about 60ml/4 tbsp of the stock, and set aside.

3 Heat the oil in a preheated wok or large frying pan. Add the garlic, ginger and spring onions and stir-fry for a few seconds.

4 Add the seafood and wine and stir-fry for 1 minute. Add the reserved stock and simmer for 2 minutes.

5 Mix together the cornflour and water to a smooth paste. Add the mixture to the wok or pan and cook, stirring gently, until the sauce thickens.

6 Season with salt and pepper to taste. Transfer to a serving dish and serve immediately with noodles.

—— COOK'S TIP ——
Do not overcook the seafood or it will become rubbery.

Monkfish and Scallop Skewers

Using lemon grass stalks as skewers imbues the seafood with a subtle citrus flavour.

INGREDIENTS

Serves 4

450g/1lb monkfish fillet
8 lemon grass stalks
30ml/2 tbsp fresh lemon juice
15ml/1 tbsp olive oil
15ml/1 tbsp finely chopped
    fresh coriander
2.5ml/½ tsp salt
12 large scallops, cut in
    half crossways
freshly ground black pepper
fresh coriander sprigs, to garnish
rice, to serve

1 Remove the tough, transparent membrane from the monkfish, otherwise it will shrink during cooking. Cut the flesh into 16 large chunks with a sharp knife.

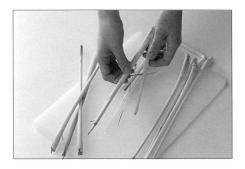

2 Remove the outer leaves from the lemon grass. Finely chop the tender parts of the leaves and place in a bowl. Stir in the lemon juice, olive oil, chopped coriander and salt and season to taste with pepper.

3 Thread the monkfish and scallop chunks on the eight lemon grass stalks. Arrange the skewers of fish and shellfish in a shallow dish and pour over the marinade, turning the skewers to coat thoroughly.

4 Cover and set aside for 1 hour. Transfer the skewers to a steamer, cover and steam over boiling water for 10 minutes, until just cooked. Garnish with coriander and serve with rice and the cooking juice poured over.

Fried Monkfish Coated with Rice Noodles

These marinated medallions of fish are coated in rice vermicelli and deep fried – they taste as good as they look.

INGREDIENTS

Serves 4
450g/1lb monkfish
5ml/1 tsp grated fresh root ginger
1 garlic clove, finely chopped
30ml/2 tbsp soy sauce
175g/6oz rice vermicelli
50g/2oz cornflour
2 eggs, beaten
salt and freshly ground black pepper
oil for deep frying
banana leaves, to serve (optional)

For the dipping sauce
30ml/2 tbsp soy sauce
30ml/2 tbsp rice vinegar
15ml/1 tbsp sugar
2 red chillies, thinly sliced
1 spring onion, thinly sliced

1 Trim the monkfish and cut into 2.5cm/1in thick medallions. Place in a dish and add the ginger, garlic and soy sauce. Mix lightly and leave to marinate for 10 minutes.

2 Meanwhile, make the dipping sauce. Combine the soy sauce, vinegar and sugar in a small saucepan. Bring to the boil. Add salt and pepper to taste. Remove from the heat, add the chillies and spring onion and set aside until required.

3 Using kitchen scissors, cut the noodles into 4cm/1½in lengths. Spread them out in a shallow bowl.

4 Coat the fish medallions in cornflour, dip in beaten egg and cover with noodles, pressing them on to the fish so that they stick.

5 Deep fry the coated fish in hot oil, 2–3 pieces at a time, until the noodle coating is fluffy, crisp and light golden brown. Drain and serve hot on banana leaves, if you like, accompanied by the dipping sauce.

Sizzling Chinese Steamed Fish

Steamed whole fish is very popular in China, and the wok is used as a steamer. In this recipe the fish is flavoured with garlic, ginger and spring onions cooked in sizzling hot oil.

INGREDIENTS

Serves 4
4 rainbow trout, about 250g/9oz each
1.5ml/¼ tsp salt
2.5ml/½ tsp sugar
2 garlic cloves, finely chopped
15ml/1 tbsp finely diced fresh root
    ginger
5 spring onions, cut into 5cm/2in
    lengths and finely shredded
60ml/4 tbsp groundnut oil
5ml/1 tsp sesame oil
45ml/3 tbsp light soy sauce
thread egg noodles and stir-fried
    vegetables, to serve

1 Make three diagonal slits on both sides of each fish and lay them on a heatproof plate. Place a small rack or trivet in a wok half-filled with water, cover and heat until just simmering.

2 Sprinkle the fish with the salt, sugar, garlic and ginger. Place the plate securely on the rack or trivet and cover. Steam gently for about 10–12 minutes, or until the flesh has turned pale pink and feels quite firm.

3 Turn off the heat, remove the lid and scatter the spring onions over the fish. Replace the lid.

4 Heat the groundnut and sesame oils in a small pan over a high heat until just smoking, then quickly pour a quarter over the spring onions on each of the fish – the shredded onions will sizzle and cook in the hot oil. Sprinkle the soy sauce over the top. Serve the fish and juices immediately with boiled noodles and stir-fried vegetables.

Sea Bass with Chinese Chives

Chinese chives are widely available in oriental supermarkets but if you are unable to buy them, use half a large Spanish onion, finely sliced, instead.

INGREDIENTS

Serves 4

2 sea bass, about 450g/1lb in total
15ml/1 tbsp cornflour
45ml/3 tbsp vegetable oil
175g/6oz Chinese chives
15ml/1 tbsp Chinese rice wine or
   dry sherry
5ml/1 tsp caster sugar
salt and ground black pepper
Chinese chives with flowerheads,
   to garnish

1 Remove the scales from the bass by scraping them with the back of a knife, working from the tail end towards the head end. Fillet the fish.

2 Cut the fillets into large chunks and dust them lightly with cornflour, salt and pepper.

3 Heat 30ml/2 tbsp of the oil in a preheated wok. When the oil is hot, toss the chunks of fish in the wok briefly to seal, then set aside. Wipe out the wok with kitchen paper.

4 Cut the Chinese chives into 5cm/2in lengths and discard the flowers. Reheat the wok and add the remaining oil, then stir-fry the Chinese chives for 30 seconds. Add the fish and rice wine or dry sherry, then bring to the boil and stir in the sugar. Serve hot, garnished with some flowering Chinese chives.

Grey Mullet with Pork

This unusual combination makes a spectacular main dish.

INGREDIENTS

Serves 4

1 grey mullet, about 900g/2lb, gutted
   and cleaned
50g/2oz lean pork
3 dried Chinese mushrooms, soaked in
   hot water for 30 minutes
2.5ml/½ tsp cornflour
30ml/2 tbsp light soy sauce
15ml/1 tbsp vegetable oil
15ml/1 tbsp finely shredded fresh
   root ginger
15ml/1 tbsp shredded spring onion
salt and freshly ground black pepper
sliced spring onion, to garnish
rice, to serve

1 Make four diagonal cuts on either side of the fish and rub with a little salt. Place the fish on a large, shallow, heatproof serving dish.

2 Cut the pork into thin strips. Place in a bowl. Drain the soaked mushrooms, remove and discard the stalks and thinly slice the caps.

3 Add the mushrooms to the pork, together with the cornflour and half the soy sauce. Stir in 5ml/1 tsp of the oil and season generously with black pepper. Arrange the pork mixture along the length of the fish. Scatter the ginger shreds over the top.

4 Cover the fish loosely with foil. Have ready a large saucepan or roasting tin with about 5cm/2in boiling water. (It should be big enough for the heatproof dish to fit inside on a metal trivet.) Place the dish in the pan or roasting tin, cover and steam over a high heat for 15 minutes.

5 Test the fish by pressing the flesh gently. If it comes away from the bone with a slight resistance, the fish is cooked. Carefully pour away any excess liquid from the dish.

6 Heat the remaining oil in a small pan. Add the shredded spring onion and stir-fry for a few seconds, then pour it over the fish, taking great care as it will splatter. Drizzle with the remaining soy sauce, garnish with sliced spring onion and serve immediately with rice.

MEAT &
POULTRY

Stir-fried Pork with Vegetables

This is a basic recipe for stir-frying any meat with any vegetables, according to seasonal availability and preference.

INGREDIENTS

Serves 4

225g/8oz pork fillet
15ml/1 tbsp light soy sauce
5ml/1 tsp light brown sugar
5ml/1 tsp Chinese rice wine or
   dry sherry
10ml/2 tsp cornflour paste
115g/4oz mangetouts
115g/4oz white mushrooms
1 carrot
1 spring onion
60ml/4 tbsp vegetable oil
5ml/1 tsp salt
stock (optional)
few drops sesame oil

1 Cut the pork into thin slices, each about the size of a postage stamp. Marinate with about 5ml/1 tsp of the soy sauce, sugar, rice wine or sherry and cornflour paste.

2 Top and tail the mangetouts. Thinly slice the mushrooms. Cut the carrot into pieces roughly the same size as the pork and cut the spring onion into short sections.

3 Heat the oil in a preheated wok and stir-fry the pork for about 1 minute or until its colour changes. Remove with a slotted spoon and keep warm while you cook the vegetables.

4 Add the vegetables to the wok and stir-fry for about 2 minutes. Add the salt and the partly cooked pork, and a little stock or water if necessary. Continue cooking and stirring for about 1 minute, then add the remaining soy sauce and blend well. Sprinkle with the sesame oil and serve.

Hot-and-sour Pork

This tasty dish is cooked in the oven and uses less oil than a stir-fry. Trim all visible fat from the pork before cooking, for a healthy, low-fat recipe.

INGREDIENTS

Serves 4

350g/12oz pork fillet
5ml/1 tsp sunflower oil
2.5cm/1in fresh root ginger, grated
1 fresh red chilli, seeded and
    finely chopped
5ml/1 tsp Chinese five-spice powder
15ml/1 tbsp sherry vinegar
15ml/1 tbsp soy sauce
225g/8oz can pineapple chunks in
    natural juice
175ml/6fl oz/¾ cup chicken stock
20ml/4 tsp cornflour
15ml/1 tbsp water
1 small green pepper, seeded and sliced
115g/4oz baby sweetcorn, halved
salt and ground black pepper
sprig of flat-leaf parsley, to garnish
boiled rice, to serve

1 Trim away any visible fat from the pork and cut into 1cm/½in-thick slices using a sharp knife.

2 Brush the sunflower oil over the base of a flameproof casserole. Heat over a medium heat, then fry the pork for about 2 minutes on each side or until lightly browned.

3 Blend together the ginger, chilli, Chinese five-spice powder, sherry vinegar and soy sauce.

4 Drain the pineapple chunks, reserving the juice. Make the stock up to 300ml/½ pint/1¼ cups with the reserved juice, mix together with the spices and pour over the pork.

5 Slowly bring the stock to the boil. Blend the cornflour with the water and gradually stir into the pork. Add the green pepper and baby sweetcorn and season to taste.

6 Cover and cook in a preheated oven at 160°C/325°F/Gas 3 for 30 minutes or until the pork is tender. Stir in the pineapple and cook for a further 5 minutes. Garnish with flat-leaf parsley and serve with boiled rice.

COOK'S TIP

Chinese five-spice powder is available from oriental food stores and some large supermarkets. However, if you cannot find it, you can use ground mixed spice instead, although the flavour will be slightly different.

Lion's Head Casserole

The name of this dish – *shi zi tou* in Chinese – derives from the rather strange idea that the meatballs look like a lion's head and the Chinese leaves resemble its mane.

INGREDIENTS

Serves 4–6
450g/1lb minced pork
10ml/2 tsp finely chopped spring onion
5ml/1 tsp finely chopped fresh root ginger
50g/2oz mushrooms, chopped
50g/2oz cooked prawns, peeled, or crab meat, finely chopped
15ml/1 tbsp light soy sauce
5ml/1 tsp light brown sugar
15ml/1 tbsp Chinese rice wine or dry sherry

15ml/1 tbsp cornflour
675g/1½lb Chinese leaves
45–60ml/3–4 tbsp vegetable oil
5ml/1 tsp salt
300ml/½ pint/1¼ cups Basic Stock or water

1 Mix together the pork, spring onion, ginger, mushrooms, prawns or crab meat, soy sauce, brown sugar, rice wine or dry sherry and cornflour. Shape the mixture into 4–6 meatballs.

2 Cut the Chinese leaves into large pieces, all about the same size.

3 Heat the oil in a preheated wok or large frying pan. Add the Chinese leaves and salt and stir-fry for 2–3 minutes. Add the meatballs and the stock, bring to the boil, cover and simmer gently for 30–45 minutes. Serve immediately.

Stir-fried Pork with Tomatoes and Courgettes

This dish is a perfect example of the Chinese way of balancing and harmonizing colours, flavours and textures.

INGREDIENTS

Serves 4
225g/8oz pork fillet, thinly sliced
15ml/1 tbsp light soy sauce
5ml/1 tsp light brown sugar
5ml/1 tsp Chinese rice wine or dry sherry
10ml/2 tsp cornflour paste
115g/4oz firm tomatoes, skinned
175g/6oz courgettes
1 spring onion
60ml/4 tbsp vegetable oil
5ml/1 tsp salt (optional)
Basic Stock or water, if necessary

1 Put the pork in a bowl with 5ml/1 tsp of the soy sauce, the sugar, rice wine or dry sherry and cornflour paste. Set aside to marinate. Cut the tomatoes and courgettes into wedges. Slice the spring onion.

2 Heat the oil in a preheated wok and stir-fry the pork for 1 minute, or until it colours. Remove with a slotted spoon, set aside and keep warm.

3 Add the vegetables to the wok and stir-fry for 2 minutes. Add the salt, if using, the pork and a little stock or water, if necessary, and stir-fry for 1 minute. Add the remaining soy sauce, mix well and serve.

Char-siu Pork

Marinated pork, roasted and glazed with honey, is irresistible on its own and can also be used as the basis for salads or stir-fries.

Ingredients

Serves 6
15ml/1 tbsp vegetable oil
15ml/1 tbsp hoisin sauce
15ml/1 tbsp yellow bean sauce
1.5ml/¼ tsp Chinese five spice powder
2.5ml/½ tsp cornflour
15ml/1 tbsp caster sugar
450g/1lb pork fillet, trimmed
10ml/2 tsp clear honey
salt and freshly ground white pepper
shredded spring onion, to garnish
boiled rice, to serve

1 Mix together the vegetable oil, hoisin sauce, yellow bean sauce, Chinese five spice powder, cornflour and sugar in a shallow dish and season to taste with salt and pepper. Add the pork to the dish and turn to coat with the marinade thoroughly. Cover and chill for 4 hours.

2 Preheat the oven to 190°C/375°F/ Gas 5. Drain the pork and place it on a wire rack over a deep roasting tin. Roast for 40 minutes, turning the pork over from time to time.

3 Check that the pork is cooked by inserting a skewer or fork into the meat; the juices should run clear. If they are still tinged with pink, roast the pork for a further 5–10 minutes.

4 Remove the pork from the oven and brush it with the honey. Allow to cool for 10 minutes before cutting into thin slices. Transfer to a serving dish, garnish with shredded spring onion and serve either hot or cold with boiled rice.

Stir-fried Pork with Lychees

Crispy pieces of pork with fleshy lychees make an unusual stir-fry that is ideal for a dinner party.

INGREDIENTS

Serves 4

450g/1lb fatty pork, such as belly pork
30ml/2 tbsp hoi-sin sauce
4 spring onions, sliced
175g/6oz lychees, peeled, stoned and
   cut into slivers
salt and ground black pepper
fresh lychees and fresh parsley sprigs, to
   garnish

1 Cut the pork into bite-sized pieces.

2 Pour the hoi-sin sauce over the pork and marinate for 30 minutes.

3 Heat the wok, then add the pork and stir-fry for 5 minutes until crisp and golden. Add the spring onions and stir-fry for a further 2 minutes.

4 Scatter the lychee slivers over the pork, and season well with salt and pepper. Garnish with fresh lychees and parsley, and serve.

COOK'S TIP

If you cannot buy fresh lychees, this dish can be made with drained canned lychees.

Spicy Meat Fritters

INGREDIENTS

Makes 30

450g/1lb potatoes, boiled and drained
450g/1lb lean minced beef
1 onion, quartered
1 bunch spring onions, chopped
3 garlic cloves, crushed
5ml/1 tsp ground nutmeg
15ml/1 tbsp coriander seeds, dry-fried
   and ground
10ml/2 tsp cumin seeds, dry-fried
   and ground
4 eggs, beaten
oil for shallow-frying
salt and freshly ground black pepper

1 While the potatoes are still warm, mash them in the pan until they are well broken up. Add to the minced beef and mix well together.

2 Finely chop the onion, spring onions and garlic. Add to the meat with the ground nutmeg, coriander and cumin. Stir in enough beaten egg to give a soft consistency which can be formed into fritters. Season to taste.

3 Heat the oil in a large frying pan. Using a dessertspoon, scoop out 6–8 oval-shaped fritters and drop them into the hot oil. Allow to set, so that they keep their shape (this will take about 3 minutes) and then turn over and cook for a further minute.

4 Drain well on kitchen paper and keep warm while cooking the remaining fritters.

Barbecued Pork Spareribs

INGREDIENTS

Serves 4

1kg/2¼ lb pork spareribs
1 onion
2 garlic cloves
2.5cm/1in fresh root ginger
75ml/3fl oz/⅓ cup dark soy sauce
1–2 fresh red chillies, seeded
   and chopped
5ml/1 tsp tamarind pulp, soaked in
   75ml/3fl oz/⅓ cup water
15–30ml/1–2 tbsp dark brown sugar
30ml/2 tbsp groundnut oil
salt and freshly ground black pepper

1 Wipe the pork ribs and place them in a wok, wide frying pan or large flameproof casserole.

2 Finely chop the onion, crush the garlic and peel and slice the ginger. Blend the soy sauce, onion, garlic, ginger and chopped chillies together to a paste in a food processor or with a pestle and mortar. Strain the tamarind and reserve the juice. Add the tamarind juice, brown sugar, oil and seasoning to taste to the onion mixture and mix well together.

3 Pour the sauce over the ribs and toss well to coat. Bring to the boil and then simmer, uncovered and stirring frequently, for 30 minutes. Add extra water if necessary.

4 Put the ribs on a rack in a roasting tin, place under a preheated grill, on a barbecue or in the oven at 200°C/400°F/Gas 6 and continue cooking until the ribs are tender, about 20 minutes, depending on the thickness of the ribs. Baste the ribs with the sauce and turn them over from time to time.

Braised Birthday Noodles with Hoisin Lamb

In China, the egg symbolizes continuity and fertility so it is frequently included in birthday dishes. The noodles traditionally served at birthday celebrations are left long: it is considered bad luck to cut them since this might shorten one's life.

INGREDIENTS

Serves 4
350g/12oz thick egg noodles
1kg/2¼lb lean neck fillets of lamb
30ml/2 tbsp vegetable oil
115g/4oz fine green beans, topped and
    tailed, and blanched
salt and freshly ground black pepper
2 hard-boiled eggs, halved, and
    2 spring onions, finely chopped,
    to garnish

For the marinade
2 garlic cloves, crushed
10ml/2 tsp grated fresh root ginger
30ml/2 tbsp soy sauce
30ml/2 tbsp rice wine
1–2 dried red chillies
30ml/2 tbsp vegetable oil

For the sauce
15ml/1 tbsp cornflour
30ml/2 tbsp soy sauce
30ml/2 tbsp rice wine
grated rind and juice of ½ orange
15ml/1 tbsp hoisin sauce
15ml/1 tbsp wine vinegar
5ml/1 tsp soft light brown sugar

1 Bring a large saucepan of water to the boil. Add the noodles and cook for 2 minutes only. Drain, rinse under cold water and drain again. Set aside.

2 Cut the lamb into 5cm/2in thick medallions. Mix the ingredients for the marinade in a large shallow dish. Add the lamb and leave to marinate for at least 4 hours or overnight.

3 Heat the oil in a heavy-based saucepan or flameproof casserole. Fry the lamb for 5 minutes until browned. Add just enough water to cover the meat. Bring to the boil, skim, then reduce the heat and simmer for 40 minutes or until the meat is tender, adding more water as necessary.

4 Make the sauce. Blend the cornflour with the remaining ingredients in a bowl. Stir into the lamb and mix well without breaking up the meat.

5 Add the noodles to the lamb with the beans. Simmer gently until both the noodles and the beans are cooked. Add salt and pepper to taste. Divide the noodles, lamb and beans among four large bowls, garnish each portion with half a hard-boiled egg, sprinkle with spring onions and serve.

Five-spice Lamb

This aromatic and mouth-watering lamb dish is perfect for an informal supper party.

INGREDIENTS

Serves 4

30ml/2 tbsp oil
1.5kg/3–3½lb leg of lamb, boned
  and cubed
1 onion, chopped
10ml/2 tsp grated fresh root ginger
1 garlic clove, crushed
5ml/1 tsp Chinese five-spice powder
30ml/2 tbsp hoisin sauce
15ml/1 tbsp light soy sauce
300ml/½ pint/1¼ cups passata
250ml/8fl oz/1 cup lamb stock
1 red pepper, seeded and diced
1 yellow pepper, seeded and diced
30ml/2 tbsp chopped fresh coriander
15ml/1 tbsp sesame seeds, toasted
salt and ground black pepper
boiled rice, to serve

1 Heat 30ml/2 tbsp of the oil in a flameproof casserole and brown the lamb in batches over a high heat. Remove and set aside.

2 Add the onion, ginger and garlic to the casserole with a little more oil, if necessary, and cook for about 5 minutes, until softened.

3 Return the lamb to the casserole. Stir in the five-spice powder, hoisin and soy sauces, passata, stock and seasoning. Bring to the boil, cover and cook in a preheated oven at 160°C/325°F/Gas 3 for 1¼ hours.

4 Remove the casserole from the oven, stir in the peppers, then cover and return to the oven for a further 15 minutes, or until the lamb is cooked and very tender.

5 Sprinkle with the coriander and sesame seeds. Serve hot with rice.

Peking Beef and Pepper Stir-fry

This quick and easy stir-fry is perfect for today's busy cook and tastes superb.

INGREDIENTS

Serves 4

350g/12oz rump or sirloin steak, sliced
  into strips
30ml/2 tbsp soy sauce
30ml/2 tbsp medium sherry
15ml/1 tbsp cornflour
5ml/1 tsp brown sugar
15ml/1 tbsp sunflower oil
15ml/1 tbsp sesame oil
1 garlic clove, finely chopped
15ml/1 tbsp grated fresh root ginger
1 red pepper, seeded and sliced
1 yellow pepper, seeded and sliced
115g/4oz sugar snap peas
4 spring onions, cut into 5cm/2in
  lengths
30ml/2 tbsp oyster sauce
60ml/4 tbsp water
cooked noodles, to serve

1 In a bowl, mix together the steak strips, soy sauce, sherry, cornflour and brown sugar. Cover and leave to marinate for 30 minutes.

2 Heat the sunflower and sesame oils in a preheated wok or large frying pan. Add the garlic and ginger and stir-fry for about 30 seconds. Add the peppers, sugar snap peas and spring onions and stir-fry for 3 minutes.

3 Add the beef, together with the marinade juices, to the wok or frying pan and stir-fry for a further 3–4 minutes. Pour in the oyster sauce and water and stir until the sauce has thickened slightly. Serve immediately with cooked noodles.

Beef with Cantonese Oyster Sauce

This is a classic Cantonese recipe in which any combination of vegetables can be used. Broccoli may be used instead of mangetouts, bamboo shoots instead of baby corn cobs, and white or black mushrooms instead of straw mushrooms, for example.

INGREDIENTS

Serves 4

275–350g/10–12oz rump steak
5ml/1 tsp light brown sugar
15ml/1 tbsp light soy sauce
10ml/2 tsp Chinese rice wine or
   dry sherry
10ml/2 tsp cornflour paste
115g/4oz mangetouts
115g/4oz baby corn cobs
115g/4oz straw mushrooms
1 spring onion
300ml/½ pint/1¼ cups vegetable oil
few small pieces of fresh root ginger
2.5ml/½ tsp salt
30ml/2 tbsp oyster sauce

1 Cut the beef into thin strips. Place in a bowl and add the sugar, soy sauce, rice wine or dry sherry and cornflour paste. Mix well and set aside to marinate for 25–30 minutes.

2 Top and tail the mangetouts and cut the baby corn cobs in half. If using canned straw mushrooms, drain them. If the straw mushrooms are large, cut them in half, but leave whole if they are small. Cut the spring onion into short sections.

3 Heat the oil in a preheated wok and stir-fry the beef until the colour changes. Remove with a perforated spoon and drain.

4 Pour off the excess oil, leaving about 30ml/2 tbsp in the wok, then add the spring onion, ginger and the vegetables. Stir-fry for about 2 minutes with the salt, then add the beef and the oyster sauce. Blend well and serve.

Beef with Peppers and Black Bean Sauce

A rich dish with the distinctive flavour of black bean sauce.

INGREDIENTS

Serves 4

350g/12oz rump steak, trimmed and
   thinly sliced
15ml/1 tbsp vegetable oil
300ml/½ pint/1¼ cups beef stock
2 garlic cloves, finely chopped
5ml/1 tsp grated fresh root ginger
1 fresh red chilli, seeded and finely
   chopped
15ml/1 tbsp black bean sauce
1 green pepper, seeded and cut into
   2.5cm/1in squares
15ml/1 tbsp dry sherry
5ml/1 tsp cornflour
5ml/1 tsp caster sugar
45ml/3 tbsp cold water
salt
rice noodles, to serve

1 **Place the steak in a bowl. Add 5ml/1 tsp of oil and stir to coat.**

2 Bring the stock to the boil in a saucepan. Add the beef and cook for 2 minutes, stirring constantly to prevent the slices from sticking together. Drain the beef and set aside.

-------- COOK'S TIP --------

For extra colour, use half each of a green pepper and red pepper or a mixture that includes yellow and orange.

3 Heat the remaining oil in a non-stick frying pan or wok. Stir-fry the garlic, ginger and chilli with the black bean sauce for a few seconds. Add the pepper squares and a little water. Cook for about 2 minutes more, then stir in the sherry. Add the beef slices to the pan and spoon the sauce over.

4 In a small bowl, mix the cornflour and sugar to a paste with the water. Pour the mixture into the pan. Cook, stirring, until the sauce has thickened. Season with salt and serve at once, with rice noodles.

Beef in Oyster Sauce

The oyster sauce gives the beef extra richness and depth of flavour. To complete the dish, all you need is plain boiled rice or simply cooked noodles.

INGREDIENTS

Serves 4

350g/12oz rump steak, thinly sliced
15ml/1 tbsp vegetable oil
300ml/½ pint/1¼ cups beef stock
2 garlic cloves, finely chopped
1 small carrot, thinly sliced
3 celery sticks, sliced
15ml/1 tbsp Chinese rice wine
5ml/1 tsp caster sugar
45ml/3 tbsp oyster sauce
5ml/1 tsp cornflour
15ml/1 tbsp water
4 spring onions, cut into 2.5cm/
    1in lengths
freshly ground white pepper
rice or noodles, to serve

1 Place the steak in a bowl, add 5ml/ 1 tsp of the oil and stir to coat.

2 Bring the stock to the boil in a large saucepan. Add the steak and cook, stirring, for 2 minutes. Drain, reserving 45ml/3 tbsp of the stock, and set aside.

3 Heat the remaining oil in a preheated wok. Stir-fry the garlic for a few seconds, then add the carrot and celery and stir-fry for 2 minutes.

4 Stir in the Chinese rice wine, caster sugar and oyster sauce and season with pepper. Add the steak to the wok, together with the reserved stock. Simmer for 2 minutes.

5 Mix together the cornflour and water to a smooth paste. Add the mixture to the wok and cook, stirring constantly, until thickened.

6 Stir in the spring onions. Transfer to a warm serving dish and serve with plain boiled rice or noodles.

Oriental Beef

This sumptuous stir-fried beef melts in the mouth, and is perfectly complemented by the delicious crunchy relish.

INGREDIENTS

Serves 4
450g/1lb rump steak
15ml/1 tbsp sunflower oil
4 whole radishes, to garnish

For the marinade
2 cloves garlic, crushed
60ml/4 tbsp dark soy sauce
30ml/2 tbsp dry sherry
10ml/2 tsp soft dark brown sugar

For the relish
6 radishes
10cm/4in piece cucumber
1 piece stem ginger

1 Cut the beef into thin strips. Place in a bowl.

2 To make the marinade, mix together the garlic, soy sauce, sherry and sugar in a bowl. Pour it over the beef and leave to marinate overnight.

─── COOK'S TIP ───

Dark soy sauce has a stronger, more robust flavour than light soy sauce. It is particularly useful for imparting a rich, dark colour to meat dishes.

3 To make the relish, chop the radishes and cucumber into short matchsticks, then cut the ginger into small matchsticks. Mix thoroughly together in a bowl.

4 Heat a wok, then add the oil. When the oil is hot, add the meat and the marinade and stir-fry for 3–4 minutes. Serve with the relish, and garnish with a whole radish on each plate.

Mandarin Sesame Duck

Duck is a high-fat meat but it is possible to get rid of a considerable proportion of the fat by cooking it in this way. (If you remove the skin completely, the meat can be dry.) For a special occasion, duck breasts are an excellent choice, but they are more expensive.

INGREDIENTS

Serves 4
4 duck legs or boneless breasts
30ml/2 tbsp light soy sauce
45ml/3 tbsp clear honey
15ml/1 tbsp sesame seeds
4 mandarin oranges
5ml/1 tsp cornflour
salt and ground black pepper
mixed vegetables, to serve

1 Prick the duck skin all over. If using breasts, slash the skin diagonally at intervals with a small, sharp knife.

2 Place the duck on a rack in a roasting tin and roast for 1 hour in a preheated oven at 180°C/350°F/Gas 4. Mix 15ml/1 tbsp of the soy sauce with 30ml/2 tbsp of the honey and brush over the duck. Sprinkle with sesame seeds. Roast for 15–20 minutes, until golden brown.

3 Meanwhile, grate the rind from 1 mandarin and squeeze the juice from 2. Mix together the rind, juice and cornflour, then stir in the remaining soy sauce and honey. Heat, stirring, until thickened and clear. Season to taste. Peel and slice the remaining mandarins. Serve the duck, with the mandarin slices and the sauce, accompanied by mixed vegetables.

Peking Duck

This has to be the *pièce de résistance* of any Chinese banquet. It is not too difficult to prepare and cook at home – the secret is to use duckling with a low-fat content. Also, make sure that the skin of the duck is absolutely dry before you start to cook – the drier the skin, the crispier the duck.

INGREDIENTS

Serves 6–8
2.25kg/5–5¼lb oven-ready duckling
30ml/2 tbsp maltose or honey, dissolved in 150ml/¼ pint/⅔ cup warm water

For the duck sauce
30ml/2 tbsp sesame oil
90–120ml/6–8 tbsp yellow bean sauce, crushed
30–45ml/2–3 tbsp light brown sugar

To serve
20–24 thin pancakes
6–8 spring onions, thinly shredded
½ cucumber, thinly shredded

COOK'S TIP

If preferred, serve Peking Duck with plum sauce in place of the duck sauce. Plum sauce is available from oriental stores and larger supermarkets. Duck sauce can also be bought ready-prepared.

1 Remove any feather studs and any lumps of fat from inside the vent of the duck. Plunge the duck into a saucepan of boiling water for 2–3 minutes to seal the pores. This will make the skin airtight, thus preventing the fat from escaping during cooking. Remove and drain well, then dry thoroughly.

2 Brush the duck all over with the dissolved maltose or honey, then hang the bird up in a cool place for at least 4–5 hours.

3 Place the duck, breast side up, on a rack in a roasting tin and cook in a preheated oven at 200°C/400°F/Gas 6 for 1½–1¾ hours without either basting or turning.

4 Meanwhile, make the duck sauce. Heat the sesame oil in a small saucepan. Add the crushed yellow bean sauce and the light brown sugar. Stir until smooth and allow to cool.

5 To serve, peel off the crispy duck skin in small slices using a sharp carving knife or cleaver, then carve the juicy meat in thin strips. Arrange the skin and meat on separate serving plates.

6 Open a pancake on each plate, spread about 5ml/1 tsp of the chosen sauce in the middle, with a few strips of shredded spring onions and cucumber. Top with 2–3 slices each of duck skin and meat. Roll up and eat.

Sweet-sour Duck with Mango

Mango adds natural sweetness to this colourful stir-fry. Crispy deep-fried noodles make the perfect accompaniment.

INGREDIENTS

Serves 4

225–350g/8–12oz duck breasts
45ml/3 tbsp dark soy sauce
15ml/1tbsp Chinese rice wine or
  dry sherry
5ml/1 tsp sesame oil
5ml/1 tsp Chinese five-spice powder
15ml/1 tbsp soft brown sugar
10ml/2 tsp cornflour
45ml/3 tbsp Chinese rice vinegar
15ml/1 tbsp tomato ketchup
1 mango, not too ripe
3 baby aubergines
1 red onion
1 carrot
60ml/4 tbsp groundnut oil
1 garlic clove, sliced
2.5cm/1in fresh root ginger, cut
  into shreds
75g/3oz sugar snap peas

1 Thinly slice the duck breasts and place in a bowl. Mix together 15ml/1 tbsp of the soy sauce with the rice wine or sherry, sesame oil and five-spice powder. Pour over the duck, cover and leave to marinate for 1–2 hours. In a separate bowl, blend together the sugar, cornflour, rice vinegar, ketchup and remaining soy sauce. Set aside.

2 Peel the mango, slice the flesh from the stone, then cut into thick strips. Slice the aubergines, onion and carrot into similar-sized pieces.

3 Heat a wok until hot, add 30ml/ 2 tbsp of the oil and swirl it around. Drain the duck, reserving the marinade. Stir-fry the duck slices over a high heat until the fat is crisp and golden. Remove and keep warm. Add 15ml/1 tbsp of the oil to the wok and stir-fry the aubergine for 3 minutes until golden.

4 Add the remaining oil and fry the onion, garlic, ginger and carrot for 2–3 minutes, then add the sugar snap peas and stir fry for a further 2 minutes.

5 Add the mango and return the duck with the sauce and reserved marinade to the wok. Cook, stirring, until the sauce thickens slightly. Serve at once.

COOK'S TIP

If baby aubergines are not available, use the smallest you can find. Sprinkle with salt after slicing and set aside in a colander for the bitter juices to drain off. Rinse thoroughly before cooking.

Chicken with Lemon Sauce

Succulent chicken with a refreshing lemony sauce and just a hint of lime is a sure winner.

INGREDIENTS

Serves 4

4 small skinless chicken breasts fillets
5ml/1 tsp sesame oil
15ml/1 tbsp Chinese rice wine
1 egg white, lightly beaten
30ml/2 tbsp cornflour
15ml/1 tbsp vegetable oil
salt and freshly ground white pepper
coriander leaves, spring onions and
    lemon wedges, to garnish

For the sauce

45ml/3 tbsp lemon juice
30ml/2 tbsp lime cordial
45ml/3 tbsp caster sugar
10ml/2 tsp cornflour
90ml/6 tbsp water

1 Arrange the chicken breasts in a single layer in a shallow bowl. Mix together the sesame oil and Chinese rice wine and season with salt and pepper. Pour over the chicken, cover and set aside in a cool place to marinate for about 15 minutes.

2 Mix together the egg white and cornflour. Add the mixture to the chicken and turn the chicken with tongs until it is thoroughly coated. Heat the vegetable oil in a preheated wok or frying pan. Add the chicken fillets and fry, turning occasionally, for about 15 minutes, until golden brown on both sides.

3 Meanwhile, make the sauce. Combine all the ingredients in a small pan and season with salt. Bring to the boil over a low heat, stirring constantly, until the sauce is smooth and has thickened slightly.

4 Cut the chicken into bite-size pieces and arrange them on a warm serving plate. Pour the lemon sauce over, garnish with the coriander leaves, spring onions and lemon wedges and serve immediately.

Salt "Baked" Chicken

The salt crust seals in all the delicious, succulent juices, keeping the chicken moist – yet the flavour is not salty.

INGREDIENTS

Serves 8

1.5kg/3-3½lb corn-fed chicken
1.5ml/¼ tsp sea salt
2.25kg/5lb coarse rock salt
15ml/1 tbsp vegetable oil
2.5cm/1in piece fresh root ginger, finely chopped
4 spring onions, cut into thin rings
boiled rice, garnished with shredded spring onions, to serve

1 Rinse the chicken and pat dry, inside and out, with kitchen paper. Rub the inside with the sea salt.

2 Place four pieces of damp kitchen paper on the base of a heavy-based wok or frying pan just large enough to hold the chicken.

3 Sprinkle a layer of rock salt over the kitchen paper, about 1cm/½in thick. Place the chicken on top.

4 Pour the remaining salt over the chicken until it is completely covered. Dampen six more pieces of kitchen paper and place them around the rim of the wok or frying pan. Cover with a tight-fitting lid. Put the wok or frying pan over a high heat for 10 minutes, or until it gives off a slightly smoky smell.

5 Immediately reduce the heat to medium and continue to cook the chicken for 30 minutes without lifting the lid. Then turn off the heat and leave for a further 10 minutes before carefully lifting the chicken out of the salt. Brush off any salt still clinging to the chicken and allow it to cool for 20 minutes before cutting it into serving-size pieces.

6 Heat the oil in a small saucepan until it is very hot. Add the ginger and spring onions and fry for a few seconds, then pour into a heatproof bowl and use as a dipping sauce for the chicken. Transfer the chicken to a warm serving plate and serve immediately with boiled rice, garnished with shredded spring onions.

Chicken and Cashew Nut Stir-fry

Hoi-sin sauce lends a sweet yet slightly hot note to this chicken stir-fry, while cashew nuts add a pleasing contrast of texture.

Ingredients

Serves 4

75g/3oz cashew nuts
1 red pepper
450g/1lb skinless chicken breast fillets
45ml/3 tbsp groundnut oil
4 garlic cloves, finely chopped
30ml/2 tbsp Chinese rice wine or
  dry sherry
45ml/3 tbsp hoi-sin sauce
10ml/2 tsp sesame oil
5–6 spring onions, green parts only, cut
  into 2.5cm/1in lengths

2 Cut the red pepper in half and remove the core and seeds. Slice into thin strips. Cut the chicken fillet into thin finger-length strips.

4 Add the rice wine or sherry and hoi-sin sauce. Continue to stir-fry until the chicken is tender and all the ingredients are evenly glazed.

1 Heat a wok until hot, add the cashew nuts and dry fry over a low to medium heat for 1–2 minutes until golden brown. Remove and set aside.

3 Heat the wok again until hot, add the oil and swirl it around. Add the garlic and let it sizzle in the oil for a few seconds. Add the pepper and chicken and stir-fry for 2 minutes.

5 Stir in the sesame oil, toasted cashew nuts and spring onion tips. Serve immediately.

Cook's Tip

Use blanched almonds instead of cashew nuts, if you prefer. If you prefer a slightly less sweet taste, you could substitute light soy sauce for the hoi-sin sauce.

Fu-yung Chicken

Because the egg whites mixed with milk are deep fried in a wok, they have prompted some imaginative cooks to refer to this dish as "Deep Fried Milk"!

INGREDIENTS

Serves 4
175g/6oz chicken breast fillet, skinned
5ml/1 tsp salt
4 egg whites, lightly beaten
15ml/1 tbsp cornflour paste, see page 30
30ml/2 tbsp milk
vegetable oil, for deep frying
1 lettuce heart, separated into leaves
about 120ml/4fl oz/¹/₂ cup stock
15ml/1 tbsp Chinese rice wine or
  dry sherry
15ml/1 tbsp green peas
few drops sesame oil
5ml/1 tsp minced ham, to garnish

1 Finely mince the chicken meat, then mix with a pinch of the salt, the egg whites, cornflour paste and milk. Blend well until smooth.

2 Heat the oil in a very hot wok, but before the oil gets too hot, gently spoon the chicken and egg white mixture into the oil in batches. Do not stir, otherwise it will scatter. Stir the oil from the bottom of the wok so that the egg whites will rise to the surface. Remove as soon as the colour turns bright white. Drain.

3 Pour off the excess oil, leaving about 15ml/1 tbsp in the wok. Stir-fry the lettuce leaves with the remaining salt for 1 minute, add the stock and bring to the boil.

4 Add the chicken to the wok with the rice wine and peas, and blend well. Sprinkle with sesame oil, garnish with ham and serve immediately.

Stir-fried Turkey with Mangetouts

Turkey is often a rather disappointing meat with a bland flavour. Here it is enlivened with a delicious marinade and combined with crunchy nuts to provide contrasting textures.

INGREDIENTS

Serves 4
30ml/2 tbsp sesame oil
90ml/6 tbsp lemon juice
1 garlic clove, crushed
1cm/½in fresh root ginger, grated
5ml/1 tsp clear honey
450g/1lb turkey fillets, skinned and cut
   into strips
115g/4oz mangetouts
30ml/2 tbsp groundnut oil
50g/2oz cashew nuts
6 spring onions, cut into strips
225g/8oz can water chestnuts, drained
   and thinly sliced
salt
saffron rice, to serve

3 Drain the marinade from the turkey strips and reserve the marinade. Heat the groundnut oil in a preheated wok or large frying pan, add the cashew nuts and stir-fry for about 1–2 minutes, until golden brown. Remove the cashew nuts from the wok or frying pan, using a slotted spoon, and set aside.

4 Add the turkey to the wok or frying pan and stir-fry for 3–4 minutes, until golden brown. Add the spring onions, mangetouts, water chestnuts and reserved marinade. Cook for a few minutes, until the turkey is tender and the sauce is bubbling and hot. Stir in the cashew nuts and serve with saffron rice.

1 Mix together the sesame oil, lemon juice, garlic, ginger and honey in a shallow, non-metallic dish. Add the turkey and mix well. Cover and leave to marinate for 3–4 hours.

2 Blanch the mangetouts in boiling salted water for 1 minute. Drain, refresh under cold running water and set aside.

VEGETABLES

Stir-fried Greens

Quail's eggs look very attractive in *Chah Kang Kung*, but you can substitute some baby sweetcorn, halved at an angle.

INGREDIENTS

Serves 4

2 bunches spinach or chard or 1 head Chinese leaves or 450g/1lb curly kale
3 garlic cloves, crushed
5cm/2in fresh root ginger, peeled and cut in matchsticks
45–60ml/3–4 tbsp groundnut oil
115g/4oz boneless, skinless chicken breast, or pork fillet, or a mixture of both, very finely sliced
12 quail's eggs, hard-boiled and shelled
1 fresh red chilli, seeded and shredded
30–45ml/2–3 tbsp oyster sauce
15ml/1 tbsp brown sugar
10ml/2 tsp cornflour, mixed with 50ml/2fl oz/¼ cup cold water
salt

--- COOK'S TIP ---

As with all stir-fries, don't start cooking until you have prepared all the ingredients and arranged them to hand. Cut everything into small, even-size pieces so the food can be cooked very quickly and all the colours and flavours preserved.

1 Wash the chosen leaves well and shake them dry. Strip the tender leaves from the stems and tear them into pieces. Discard the lower, tougher part of the stems and slice the remainder evenly.

2 Fry the garlic and ginger in the hot oil, without browning, for a minute. Add the chicken and/or pork and keep stirring it in the wok until the meat changes colour. When the meat looks cooked, add the sliced stems first and cook them quickly; then add the torn leaves, quail's eggs and chilli. Spoon in the oyster sauce and a little boiling water, if necessary. Cover and cook for 1–2 minutes only.

3 Remove the cover, stir and add sugar and salt to taste. Stir in the cornflour and water mixture and toss thoroughly. Cook until the mixture is well coated in a glossy sauce.

4 Serve immediately, while still very hot and the colours are bright and positively jewel-like.

Stir-fried Chinese Leaves

This really simple way of cooking Chinese leaves perfectly preserves their delicate flavour, texture and colour.

INGREDIENTS

Serves 4

675g/1½lb Chinese leaves
15ml/1 tbsp vegetable oil
2 garlic cloves, finely chopped
2.5cm/1in piece fresh root ginger, finely chopped
15ml/1 tbsp oyster sauce
4 spring onions, cut into 2.5cm/ 1in lengths
salt

1 Stack the Chinese leaves together and cut them into 2.5cm/1in slices with a sharp knife.

2 Heat the oil in a preheated wok or heavy-based frying pan. Add the garlic and ginger and stir-fry for about 1 minute.

3 Add the Chinese leaves and stir-fry for 2 minutes. Sprinkle with salt and drizzle with the oyster sauce. Toss the leaves over the heat for a further 2 minutes.

4 Stir in the spring onions. Toss the mixture well, transfer to a warm serving plate and serve.

COOK'S TIP

For vegetarians, substitute 15ml/1 tbsp light soy sauce and 5ml/1 tsp caster sugar for the oyster sauce.

Mixed Vegetables Monk-style

Chinese monks eat neither fish nor meat, so "monk-style" dishes are fine for vegetarians.

INGREDIENTS

Serves 4

50g/2oz dried bean curd sticks
115g/4oz fresh lotus root or 50g/2oz dried
10g/¼ oz dried wood ears
8 dried Chinese mushrooms
15ml/1 tbsp vegetable oil
75g/3oz/¾ cup drained, canned straw mushrooms
115g/4oz/1 cup baby corn cobs, cut in half
30ml/2 tbsp light soy sauce
15ml/1 tbsp Chinese rice wine
10ml/2 tsp caster sugar
150ml/¼ pint/⅔ cup vegetable stock
75g/3oz mangetouts, trimmed and cut in half
5ml/1 tsp cornflour
15ml/1 tbsp water
salt

1 Put the bean curd sticks in a bowl. Cover with hot water and set aside to soak for 1 hour. If using fresh lotus root, peel and slice it. If using dried lotus root, place it in a bowl of hot water and set aside to soak for 1 hour.

2 Soak the wood ears and dried mushrooms in separate bowls of hot water for 15 minutes. Drain the wood ears, discard the hard bases and cut the rest into bite-size pieces. Drain the mushrooms, trim off and discard the hard stems and chop the caps roughly.

3 Drain the bean curd sticks. Cut them into 5cm/2in long pieces, discarding any hard pieces. If using dried lotus root, drain well.

4 Heat the oil in a preheated wok or frying pan. Add the wood ears, Chinese mushrooms and lotus root and stir-fry for about 30 seconds.

5 Add the pieces of bean curd sticks, straw mushrooms, baby corn cobs, soy sauce, rice wine, caster sugar and stock. Bring to the boil, cover, lower the heat and simmer for 20 minutes.

6 Stir in the mangetouts and season to taste with salt. Mix together the cornflour and water to a smooth paste. Add the mixture to the wok or frying pan and cook, stirring constantly, until the sauce thickens. Serve immediately.

Szechuan Aubergines

INGREDIENTS

Serves 4

2 small aubergines
5ml/1 tsp salt
3 dried red chillies
groundnut oil, for deep frying
3–4 garlic cloves, finely chopped
1cm/½in fresh root ginger,
  finely chopped
4 spring onions, chopped and white
  and green parts separated
15ml/1 tbsp Chinese rice wine or
  dry sherry
15ml/1 tbsp light soy sauce
5ml/1 tsp sugar
1.5ml/¼ tsp ground roasted
  Szechuan peppercorns
15ml/1 tbsp Chinese rice vinegar
5ml/1 tsp sesame oil

1 Trim the aubergines and cut into strips, about 4cm/1½in wide and 7.5cm/3in long. Place the aubergines in a colander and sprinkle with the salt. Leave for 30 minutes, then rinse them thoroughly under cold running water. Pat dry with kitchen paper.

2 Meanwhile soak the chillies in warm water for 15 minutes. Drain, then cut each chilli into three or four pieces, discarding the seeds.

3 Half-fill a wok with oil and heat to 180°C/350°F. Deep fry the aubergine until golden brown. Drain on kitchen paper. Pour off most of the oil from the wok. Reheat the oil and add the garlic, ginger and white part of the spring onions.

4 Stir-fry for 30 seconds. Add the aubergine and toss, then add the wine or sherry, soy sauce, sugar, ground Szechuan peppercorns and rice vinegar. Stir-fry for 1–2 minutes. Sprinkle over the sesame oil and green spring onion.

Root Vegetables with Spiced Salt

All kinds of root vegetables can be finely sliced and deep fried to make "crisps". Serve as an accompaniment to an oriental-style meal or simply by themselves as much tastier nibbles than commercial snacks with pre-dinner drinks.

INGREDIENTS

Serves 4–6
1 carrot
2 parsnips
2 raw beetroots
1 sweet potato
groundnut oil, for deep frying
1.5ml/¼ tsp chilli powder
5ml/1 tsp sea salt flakes

1 Peel the carrot, parsnips, beetroots and sweet potato. Slice the carrot and parsnips into long, thin ribbons. Cut the beetroots and sweet potato into thin rounds. Pat dry on kitchen paper.

2 Half-fill a wok with oil and heat to 180°C/350°F. Add the vegetable slices in batches and deep-fry for 2–3 minutes until golden and crisp. Remove and drain on kitchen paper.

3 Place the chilli powder and sea salt flakes in a mortar and grind them together with a pestle to form a coarse powder.

4 Pile up the vegetable "crisps" on a serving plate and sprinkle over the spiced salt.

COOK'S TIP

To save time, you can slice the vegetables using a mandoline, blender or food processor with a thin slicing disc attached.

Red-cooked Tofu with Chinese Mushrooms

Red-cooked is a term applied to Chinese dishes cooked with a dark soy sauce. This tasty dish can be served as either a side dish or main meal.

INGREDIENTS

Serves 4

225g/8oz firm tofu
45ml/3 tbsp dark soy sauce
30ml/2 tbsp Chinese rice wine or dry sherry
10ml/2 tsp soft dark brown sugar
1 garlic clove, crushed
15ml/1 tbsp grated fresh root ginger
2.5ml/½ tsp Chinese five-spice powder
pinch of ground roasted Szechuan peppercorns
6 dried Chinese black mushrooms
5ml/1 tsp cornflour
30ml/2 tbsp groundnut oil
5–6 spring onions, sliced into 2.5cm/1in lengths, white and green parts separated
small fresh basil leaves, to garnish
rice noodles, to serve

2 Meanwhile soak the dried black mushrooms in warm water for 20–30 minutes until soft. Drain, reserving 90ml/6 tbsp of the soaking liquid. Squeeze out any excess liquid from the mushrooms, remove the tough stalks and slice the caps. In a small bowl, blend the cornflour with the reserved marinade and mushroom soaking liquid.

4 Add the mushrooms and white parts of the spring onions to the wok and stir-fry for 2 minutes. Pour in the marinade mixture and stir for 1 minute until thickened.

5 Return the tofu to the wok with the green parts of the spring onions. Simmer gently for 1–2 minutes. Scatter over the basil leaves and serve at once with rice noodles.

1 Drain the tofu, pat dry with kitchen paper and cut into 2.5cm/1in cubes. Place in a shallow dish. In a small bowl, mix together the soy sauce, rice wine or sherry, sugar, garlic, ginger, five-spice powder and Szechuan peppercorns. Pour the marinade over the tofu, toss well and leave to marinate for about 30 minutes. Drain, reserving the marinade.

3 Heat a wok until hot, add the oil and swirl it around. Add the tofu and stir-fry for 2–3 minutes until evenly golden. Remove from the wok and set aside.

Braised Chinese Vegetables

The original recipe calls for no less than 18 different ingredients to represent the 18 Buddhas (*Lo Han*). Later, this was reduced to eight, but nowadays anything between four and six items is regarded as quite sufficient to put in a wok.

INGREDIENTS

Serves 4

10g/¼oz dried Chinese mushrooms
75g/3oz straw mushrooms
75g/3oz sliced bamboo shoots, drained
50g/2oz mangetouts
1 packet tofu
175g/6oz Chinese leaves
45–60ml/3–4 tbsp vegetable oil
5ml/1 tsp salt
2.5ml/½ tsp light brown sugar
15ml/1 tbsp light soy sauce
few drops sesame oil

1 Soak the Chinese mushrooms in cold water for 20–25 minutes, then rinse and discard the hard stalks, if any. Cut the straw mushrooms in half lengthways, if they are large, keep them whole, if they are small. Rinse and drain the bamboo shoot slices. Top and tail the mangetouts. Cut the tofu into about 12 small pieces. Cut the Chinese leaves into small pieces about the same size as the mangetouts.

2 Harden the tofu pieces by placing them in a wok of boiling water for about 2 minutes. Remove and drain.

3 Discard the water and heat the oil in the wok. a saucepan or a flameproof casserole. Lightly brown the tofu pieces on both sides. Remove with a slotted spoon and keep warm.

4 Stir-fry all the vegetables in the wok or pan for about 1½ minutes, then add the tofu, salt, sugar and soy sauce. Continue stirring for 1 minute, then cover and braise for 2–3 minutes. Sprinkle with sesame oil and serve.

Stir-fried Beansprouts

This is an easy way to cook up some tasty beansprouts in a wok. It is not necessary to top and tail them. Simply rinse in a bowl of cold water and discard any husks that float to the surface.

INGREDIENTS

Serves 4

2–3 spring onions
225g/8oz fresh beansprouts
45ml/3 tbsp vegetable oil
5ml/1 tsp salt
2.5ml/½ tsp light brown sugar
few drops sesame oil (optional)

1 Cut the spring onions into short sections about the same length as the beansprouts.

2 Heat the oil in a wok and stir-fry the beansprouts and spring onions for about 1 minute. Add the salt and sugar and continue stirring for 1 minute. Sprinkle with the sesame oil, if using, and serve. Do not overcook or the beansprouts will go soggy.

COOK'S TIP

Fresh and canned bean sprouts are readily available, but they can easily be grown at home for a constant and completely fresh supply. Scatter mung beans on several layers of damp kitchen paper on a small plate. Keep moist in a fairly warm place and the beans will sprout in a few days.

Pancakes with Stir-fried Vegetables

To serve, each person spreads a little hoi-sin sauce over a pancake, adds a helping of the filling from the wok and rolls up the pancake.

INGREDIENTS

Serves 4

3 eggs
30ml/2 tbsp water
60ml/4 tbsp groundnut oil
25g/1oz dried Chinese black
 mushrooms
25g/1oz dried wood ears
10ml/2 tsp cornflour
30ml/2 tbsp light soy sauce
30ml/2 tbsp Chinese rice wine or
 dry sherry
10ml/2 tsp sesame oil
2 garlic cloves, finely chopped
1cm/½ in fresh root ginger, cut into
 thin shreds
75g/3oz canned sliced bamboo shoots,
 drained and rinsed
175g/6oz beansprouts
4 spring onions, finely shredded
salt and ground black pepper
Chinese pancakes and hoi-sin sauce,
 to serve

1 Whisk the eggs, water and seasoning in a small bowl. Heat 15ml/1 tbsp of the groundnut oil in a wok and swirl it around. Pour in the eggs, then tilt the wok so that they spread to an even layer. Continue to cook over a high heat for about 2 minutes until set. Turn on to a board and, when cool, roll up and cut into thin strips. Wipe the wok clean.

—————— COOK'S TIP ——————

Chinese pancakes are available from oriental supermarkets. Reheat them in a bamboo steamer for 2–3 minutes just before serving.

2 Meanwhile put the black mushrooms and wood ears into separate bowls. Pour over enough warm water to cover, then leave to soak for 20–30 minutes until soft. Drain the dried mushrooms, reserving their soaking liquid. Squeeze the excess liquid from each of them.

3 Remove the tough stalks and thinly slice the black mushrooms. Finely shred the wood ears. Set aside. Strain the reserved soaking liquid through muslin into a jug; reserve 120ml/4fl oz/½ cup of the liquid. In a bowl, blend the cornflour with the reserved liquid, soy sauce, rice wine or sherry and sesame oil.

4 Heat the wok over a medium heat, add the remaining groundnut oil and swirl it around. Add the wood ears and black mushrooms and stir-fry for about 2 minutes. Add the garlic, ginger, bamboo shoots and beansprouts and stir-fry for 1–2 minutes.

5 Pour in the cornflour mixture and cook, stirring, for 1 minute until thickened. Add the spring onions and omelette strips and toss gently. Adjust the seasoning, adding more soy sauce, if needed. Serve at once with the Chinese pancakes and hoi-sin sauce.

RICE &
NOODLES

Chinese Special Fried Rice

This recipe combines a tasty mixture of chicken, prawns and vegetables with fried rice.

INGREDIENTS

Serves 4

175g/6oz/scant 1 cup long-grain white rice
45ml/3 tbsp groundnut oil
350ml/12fl oz/1½ cups water
1 garlic clove, crushed
4 spring onions, finely chopped
115g/4oz cooked chicken, diced
115g/4oz cooked prawns, peeled
50g/2oz frozen peas
1 egg, lightly beaten
50g/2oz lettuce, shredded
30ml/2 tbsp light soy sauce
pinch of caster sugar
salt and ground black pepper
15ml/1 tbsp chopped roasted cashew nuts, to garnish

1 Rinse the rice in two to three changes of warm water to wash away some of the starch. Drain well.

2 Put the rice in a saucepan and add 15ml/1 tbsp of the oil and the water. Cover and bring to the boil, stir once, then cover and simmer for 12–15 minutes, until nearly all the water has been absorbed. Turn off the heat and leave, covered, to stand for 10 minutes. Fluff up with a fork and leave to cool.

3 Heat the remaining oil in a preheated wok or frying pan, add the garlic and spring onions and stir-fry for 30 seconds.

4 Add the chicken, prawns and peas and stir-fry for 1–2 minutes, then add the cooked rice and stir-fry for a further 2 minutes. Pour in the egg and stir-fry until just set. Stir in the lettuce, soy sauce, sugar and seasoning.

5 Transfer to a warmed serving bowl, sprinkle with the chopped cashew nuts and serve immediately.

Chinese Jewelled Rice

This rice dish, with its many different, interesting ingredients, can make a meal in itself.

INGREDIENTS

Serves 4

350g/12oz long grain rice
45ml/3 tbsp vegetable oil
1 onion, roughly chopped
115g/4oz cooked ham, diced
175g/6oz canned white crab meat
75g/3oz canned water chestnuts, drained and cut into cubes
4 dried black Chinese mushrooms, soaked, drained and diced
115g/4oz peas, thawed if frozen
30ml/2 tbsp oyster sauce
5ml/1 tsp sugar
salt

1 Rinse the rice, then cook for 10–12 minutes in 700–900ml/ 1¼–1½ pints/3–3¾ cups salted water in a saucepan with a tight-fitting lid. When cooked, refresh under cold water. Heat half the oil in a preheated wok, then stir-fry the rice for 3 minutes. Remove and set aside.

2 Add the remaining oil to the wok. When the oil is hot, cook the onion until softened but not coloured.

3 Add all the remaining ingredients and stir-fry for 2 minutes.

4 Return the rice to the wok and stir-fry for 3 minutes, then serve.

Shiitake Fried Rice

Shiitake mushrooms have a strong, meaty, mushroomy aroma and flavour. This is a very easy recipe to make, and although it is a side dish, it can almost be a meal in itself.

INGREDIENTS

Serves 4
2 eggs
15ml/1 tbsp water
45ml/3 tbsp vegetable oil
350g/12oz shiitake mushrooms
8 spring onions, sliced diagonally
1 garlic clove, crushed
½ green pepper, seeded and chopped
25g/1oz/2 tbsp butter
175–225g/6–8oz/about 1 cup long-grain rice, cooked
15ml/1 tbsp medium-dry sherry
30ml/2 tbsp dark soy sauce
15ml/1 tbsp chopped fresh coriander
salt

1 Beat the eggs with the water and season with a little salt.

2 Heat 15ml/1 tbsp of the oil in a preheated wok or large frying pan, pour in the eggs and cook to make a large omelette. Lift the sides of the omelette and tilt the wok so that the uncooked egg can run underneath and be cooked. Roll up the omelette and slice thinly.

3 Remove and discard the mushroom stalks, if they are tough. Slice the caps thinly, halving them if they are large.

4 Heat 15ml/1 tbsp of the remaining oil in the wok and stir-fry the spring onions and garlic for 3–4 minutes until softened but not brown. Transfer them to a plate using a slotted spoon and set aside.

5 Add the green pepper and stir-fry for about 2–3 minutes, then add the butter and the remaining oil. As the butter begins to sizzle, add the mushrooms and stir-fry over a moderate heat for 3–4 minutes until both vegetables are soft.

6 Loosen the rice grains as much as possible. Pour the sherry over the mushrooms and then stir in the rice.

7 Heat the rice over a moderate heat, stirring all the time to prevent it sticking. If the rice seems very dry, add a little more oil. Stir in the cooked spring onions, garlic and omelette slices, the soy sauce and chopped coriander. Cook for a few minutes until heated through and serve.

Chicken Chow Mein

Chow Mein is arguably the best known Chinese noodle dish in the West. Noodles are stir-fried with meat, seafood or vegetables.

INGREDIENTS

Serves 4

350g/12oz noodles
225g/8oz skinless, boneless
  chicken breasts
45ml/3 tbsp soy sauce
15ml/1 tbsp rice wine or dry sherry
15ml/1 tbsp dark sesame oil
60ml/4 tbsp vegetable oil
2 garlic cloves, finely chopped
50g/2oz mange-touts, topped
  and tailed
115g/4oz beansprouts
50g/2oz ham, finely shredded
4 spring onions, finely chopped
salt and freshly ground black pepper

1 Cook the noodles in a saucepan of boiling water until tender. Drain, rinse under cold water and drain well.

2 Slice the chicken into fine shreds about 5cm/2in in length. Place in a bowl and add 10ml/2 tsp of the soy sauce, the rice wine or sherry and sesame oil.

3 Heat half the vegetable oil in a wok or large frying pan over a high heat. When it starts smoking, add the chicken mixture. Stir-fry for 2 minutes, then transfer the chicken to a plate and keep it hot.

4 Wipe the wok clean and heat the remaining oil. Stir in the garlic, mange-touts, beansprouts and ham, stir-fry for another minute or so and add the noodles.

5 Continue to stir-fry until the noodles are heated through. Add the remaining soy sauce to taste and season with salt and pepper. Return the chicken and any juices to the noodle mixture, add the chopped spring onions and give the mixture a final stir. Serve at once.

Sesame Duck and Noodle Salad

This salad is complete in itself and makes a lovely summer lunch. The marinade is a marvellous blend of spices.

INGREDIENTS

Serves 4
2 duck breasts
15ml/1 tbsp vegetable oil
150g/5oz sugar snap peas
2 carrots, cut into 7.5cm/3in sticks
225g/8oz medium egg noodles
6 spring onions, sliced
salt
fresh coriander leaves, to garnish

For the marinade
15ml/1 tbsp sesame oil
5ml/1 tsp ground coriander
5ml/1 tsp Chinese five-spice powder

For the dressing
15ml/1 tbsp garlic vinegar
5ml/1 tsp soft light brown sugar
5ml/1 tsp soy sauce
15ml/1 tbsp toasted sesame seeds
45ml/3 tbsp sunflower oil
30ml/2 tbsp sesame oil
ground black pepper

1 Slice the duck breasts thinly across and place them in a shallow dish. Mix all the ingredients for the marinade, pour over the duck and mix well to coat thoroughly. Cover and leave in a cool place for 30 minutes.

2 Heat the oil in a preheated wok or frying pan, add the slices of duck breast and stir-fry for 3–4 minutes until cooked. Set aside.

3 Bring a saucepan of lightly salted water to the boil. Place the sugar snap peas and carrots in a steamer that will fit on top of the pan. When the water boils, add the noodles, place the steamer on top and steam the vegetables while cooking the noodles

for the time suggested on the packet. Set the steamed vegetables aside. Drain the noodles, refresh them under cold running water and drain again. Place them in a large serving bowl.

4 Make the dressing. Mix the vinegar, sugar, soy sauce and sesame seeds in a bowl. Season well with black pepper, then whisk in the sunflower and sesame oils.

5 Pour the dressing over the noodles and mix well. Add the sugar snap peas, carrots, spring onions and duck slices and toss to mix. Scatter over the coriander leaves and serve.

Oriental Vegetable Noodles

Thin Italian egg pasta is a good
alternative to oriental egg
noodles; use it fresh or dried.

INGREDIENTS

Serves 6
500g/1¼lb thin tagliarini
1 red onion
115g/4oz shiitake mushrooms
45ml/3 tbsp sesame oil
45ml/3 tbsp dark soy sauce
15ml/1 tbsp balsamic vinegar
10ml/2 tsp caster sugar
salt
celery leaves, to garnish

1 Cook the tagliarini in a large pan
of salted boiling water, following
the instructions on the pack.

2 Thinly slice the red onion and the
mushrooms, using a sharp knife.

3 Heat 15ml/1 tbsp of the sesame oil
in a preheated wok. When the oil is
hot, stir-fry the onion and mushrooms
for 2 minutes.

4 Drain the tagliarini, then add to
the wok with the soy sauce,
balsamic vinegar, sugar and salt to taste.
Stir-fry for 1 minute, then add the
remaining sesame oil, and serve
garnished with celery leaves.

Peanut Noodles

Add any of your favourite vegetables to this recipe to make a great, quick mid-week supper – and increase the chilli, if you can take the heat!

INGREDIENTS

Serves 4
200g/7oz medium egg noodles
30ml/2 tbsp olive oil
2 garlic cloves, crushed
1 large onion, roughly chopped
1 red pepper, seeded and roughly chopped
1 yellow pepper, seeded and roughly chopped
350g/12oz courgettes, roughly chopped
150g/5oz/1¼ cups roasted unsalted peanuts, roughly chopped

For the dressing
50ml/2 fl oz/¼ cup olive oil
grated rind and juice of 1 lemon
1 fresh red chilli, seeded and finely chopped
60ml/4 tbsp chopped fresh chives
15–30ml/1–2 tbsp balsamic vinegar
salt and ground black pepper

1 Soak the noodles according to the packet instructions and drain well.

2 Meanwhile, heat the oil in a preheated wok or very large frying pan and cook the garlic and onion for 3 minutes, or until beginning to soften. Add the peppers and courgettes and cook for a further 15 minutes over a medium heat until beginning to soften and brown. Add the peanuts and cook for a further 1 minute.

3 For the dressing, whisk together the olive oil, grated lemon rind and 45ml/3 tbsp lemon juice, the chilli, 45ml/3 tbsp of the chives, plenty of seasoning and balsamic vinegar to taste.

4 Toss the noodles into the vegetables and stir-fry to heat through. Add the dressing, stir to coat and serve immediately, garnished with the remaining chopped fresh chives.

Chinese Mushrooms with Cellophane Noodles

Red fermented bean curd adds extra flavour to this hearty vegetarian dish. It is brick red in colour, with a very strong, cheesy flavour, and is made by fermenting bean curd (tofu) with salt, red rice and rice wine. Look out for it in cans or earthenware pots at Chinese food markets.

INGREDIENTS

Serves 4
115g/4oz dried Chinese mushrooms
25g/1oz dried wood ears
115g/4oz dried bean curd
30ml/2 tbsp vegetable oil
2 garlic cloves, finely chopped
2 slices fresh root ginger,
 finely chopped
10 Szechuan peppercorns, crushed
15ml/1 tbsp red fermented bean curd
½ star anise
pinch of sugar
15–30ml/1–2 tbsp soy sauce
50g/2oz cellophane noodles, soaked in
 hot water until soft
salt

1 Soak the Chinese mushrooms and wood ears separately in bowls of hot water for 30 minutes. Break the dried bean curd into small pieces and soak in water according to the instructions on the packet.

COOK'S TIP

If you can't find Szechuan peppercorns, then use ordinary black ones instead.

2 Strain the mushrooms, reserving the liquid. Squeeze as much liquid from the mushrooms as possible, then discard the mushroom stems. Cut the cups in half if they are large.

3 The wood ears should swell to five times their original size. Drain them, rinse thoroughly and drain again. Cut off any gritty parts, then cut each wood ear into two or three pieces.

4 Heat the oil in a heavy-based pan. Add the garlic, ginger and Szechuan peppercorns. Fry for a few seconds, then add the mushrooms and red fermented bean curd. Mix lightly and fry for 5 minutes.

5 Add the reserved mushroom liquid to the pan, with sufficient water to completely cover the mushrooms. Add the star anise, sugar and soy sauce, then cover and simmer for 30 minutes.

6 Add the chopped wood ears and reconstituted bean curd pieces to the pan. Cover and cook for about 10 minutes.

7 Drain the cellophane noodles, add them to the mixture and cook for a further 10 minutes until tender, adding more liquid if necessary. Add salt to taste and serve.

Fried Cellophane Noodles

INGREDIENTS

Serves 4

175g/6oz cellophane noodles
45ml/3 tbsp vegetable oil
3 garlic cloves, finely chopped
115g/4oz cooked prawns, peeled
2 lap cheong, rinsed, drained and
  finely diced
2 eggs
2 celery sticks, including leaves, diced
115g/4oz beansprouts
115g/4oz spinach, cut into
  large pieces
2 spring onions, chopped
15–30ml/1–2 tbsp fish sauce
5ml/1 tsp sesame oil
15ml/1 tbsp sesame seeds, toasted,
  to garnish

1 Soak the cellophane noodles in hot water for about 10 minutes or until soft. Drain and cut the noodles into 10cm/4in lengths.

2 Heat the oil in a wok, add the garlic and fry until golden brown. Add the prawns and lap cheong; stir-fry for 2–3 minutes. Stir in the noodles and fry for 2 minutes more.

3 Make a well in the centre of the prawn mixture, break in the eggs and slowly stir them until they are creamy and just set.

— COOK'S TIP —

This is a very versatile dish. Vary the vegetables if you wish and substitute ham, chorizo or salami for the lap cheong.

4 Stir in the celery, beansprouts, spinach and spring onions. Season with fish sauce and stir in the sesame oil. Continue to stir-fry until all the ingredients are cooked, mixing well.

5 Transfer to a serving dish. Sprinkle with sesame seeds to garnish.

DESSERTS

Chinese Fruit Salad

For an unusual fruit salad with an oriental flavour, try this mixture of fruits in a tangy lime and lychee syrup, topped with a light sprinkling of toasted sesame seeds.

INGREDIENTS

Serves 4
115g/4oz/½ cup caster sugar
300ml/½ pint/1¼ cups water
thinly pared rind and juice of 1 lime
400g/14oz can lychees in syrup
1 ripe mango, peeled, stoned and sliced
1 eating apple, cored and sliced
2 bananas, chopped
1 star fruit, sliced (optional)
5ml/1 tsp sesame seeds, toasted

1 Place the sugar in a saucepan with the water and the lime rind. Heat gently until the sugar dissolves, then increase the heat and boil gently for about 7–8 minutes. Remove from the heat and set aside to cool.

2 Drain the lychees and reserve the juice. Pour the juice into the cooled lime syrup with the lime juice. Place all the prepared fruit in a bowl and pour over the lime and lychee syrup. Chill for about 1 hour. Just before serving, sprinkle with toasted sesame seeds.

COOK'S TIP

To prepare a mango, cut through the fruit lengthways, about 1cm/½in either side of the centre. Then, using a sharp knife, cut the flesh from the central piece from the stone. Make even criss-cross cuts in the flesh of both side pieces. Hold one side piece in both hands, bend it almost inside out and remove the cubes of flesh with a spoon. Repeat with the other side piece.

Thin Pancakes

Thin pancakes are not too difficult to make, but quite a lot of practice and patience are needed to achieve the perfect result. Nowadays, even restaurants buy frozen, ready-made ones from Chinese supermarkets. If you decide to use ready-made pancakes, or are reheating home-made ones, steam them for about 5 minutes, or microwave on high (650 watts) for 1–2 minutes.

INGREDIENTS

Makes 24–30
450g/1lb/4 cups plain flour, plus extra for dusting
about 300ml/½ pint/1¼ cups boiling water
5ml/1 tsp vegetable oil

1 Sift the flour into a mixing bowl, then pour in the boiling water very gently, stirring as you pour. Mix with the oil and knead the mixture into a firm dough. Cover with a damp cloth and let stand for about 30 minutes.

2 Lightly dust a work surface with flour. Knead the dough for about 5–8 minutes, or until smooth, then divide it into 3 equal portions. Roll out each portion into a long "sausage", cut each into 8–10 pieces and roll each into a ball. Using the palm of your hand, press each piece into a flat pancake. With a rolling pin, gently roll each into a 15cm/6in circle.

3 Heat an ungreased frying pan until hot, then reduce the heat to low and place the pancakes, one at a time, in the pan. Remove the pancakes when small brown spots appear on the underside. Keep under a damp cloth until all the pancakes are cooked.

Red Bean Paste Pancakes

If you are unable to find red bean paste, sweetened chestnut purée or mashed dates are possible substitutes.

INGREDIENTS

Serves 4
about 120ml/8 tbsp sweetened red bean paste
8 Thin Pancakes
30–45ml/2–3 tbsp vegetable oil
granulated or caster sugar, to serve

1 Spread about 15ml/1 tbsp of the red bean paste over about three-quarters of each pancake, then roll the pancake over three or four times.

2 Heat the oil in a preheated wok or frying pan and fry the pancake rolls until golden brown, turning once.

3 Cut each pancake roll into three or four pieces and sprinkle with sugar to serve.

Almond Curd Junket

Also known as almond float, this
is usually made from agar-agar or
isinglass, although gelatine can
also be used.

INGREDIENTS

Serves 4–6
10g/¼oz agar-agar or isinglass or
   25g/1oz gelatine powder
about 600ml/1 pint/2½ cups water
60ml/4 tbsp granulated or caster sugar
300ml/½ pint/1¼ cups milk
5ml/1 tsp almond essence
fresh or canned mixed fruit salad with
   syrup, to serve

1 In a saucepan, dissolve the agar-
agar or isinglass in about half the
water over a gentle heat. This will take
at least 10 minutes. If using gelatine,
follow the packet instructions.

2 In a separate saucepan, dissolve the
sugar in the remaining water over a
medium heat. Add the milk and the
almond essence, blending well. Do not
allow the mixture to boil.

3 Mix the milk and sugar with the agar-
agar, isinglass or gelatine mixture in
a serving bowl. When cool, place in the
refrigerator for 2–3 hours to set.

4 To serve, cut the junket into small
cubes and spoon into a serving dish
or into individual bowls. Pour the fruit
salad, with the syrup, over the junket
and serve.

Toffee Apples

Enjoy all the flavour and texture of this classic Chinese dessert without the fuss, and high fat, of deep-frying.

INGREDIENTS

Serves 6
25g/1oz/2 tbsp butter
75ml/5 tbsp water
40g/1½oz/6 tbsp plain flour
1 egg
1 dessert apple
5ml/1 tsp vegetable oil
175g/6oz/¾ cup caster sugar
5ml/1 tsp sesame seeds

1 Preheat the oven to 200°C/400°F/ Gas 6. Put the butter and water into a small saucepan and bring to the boil. Remove from the heat and add the flour all at once. Stir vigorously until the mixture forms a smooth paste which leaves the sides of the pan clean.

2 Cool the choux paste for 5 minutes, then beat in the egg, mixing thoroughly until the mixture is smooth and glossy.

3 Peel and core the apple and cut into 1cm/½in chunks. Stir into the choux paste and place teaspoonfuls on a dampened, non-stick baking sheet. Bake for 20–25 minutes, until brown and crisp on the outside, still soft inside.

4 Heat the oil in a saucepan over a low heat and add the caster sugar. Cook, without stirring, until the sugar has melted and turned golden brown. Sprinkle in the sesame seeds and remove the pan from the heat.

5 Have a bowl of iced water at hand. Add the apple pastries, a few at a time, to the caramel and toss thoroughly to coat them all over. Remove with a slotted spoon and quickly dip them in the iced water to set the caramel. Drain well, transfer to a serving dish and serve immediately. If the caramel becomes too thick before all the apple pastries have been coated, re-heat it gently over a low heat until it liquifies again.

INDEX